The New Manager's Tool Kit

21 Things You Need to Know to Hit the Ground Running

DON & SHERYL GRIMME

ᴬMACOM

AMERICAN MANAGEMENT ASSOCIATION

New York • Atlanta • Brussels • Chicago • Mexico City • San Francisco
Shanghai • Tokyo • Toronto • Washington, D. C.

This publication is designed to provide accurate and authoritative
information in regard to the subject matter covered. It is sold with
the understanding that the publisher is not engaged in rendering
legal, accounting, or other professional service. If legal advice or
other expert assistance is required, the services of a competent professional
person should be sought.

Extensive examples in Tools #1 and #2 are excerpted from
1001 Ways to Reward Employees and *1001 Ways to Energize Employees*,
both copyrighted by Bob Nelson, Ph.D., president of Nelson Motivation
Inc., and used with permission of the author. For related ideas and
resources, visit www.nelsonmotivation.com.

Library of Congress Cataloging-in-Publication Data

Grimme, Don.
   The new manager's tool kit : 21 things you need to know to hit the ground
running / Don & Sheryl Grimme.
      p. cm.
   Includes index.
   ISBN-13: 978-0-8144-1306-7
   ISBN-10: 0-8144-1306-4
   1. Management. 2. Supervision of employees. I. Grimme, Sheryl. II. Title.

   HF5549.12.G75 2008
   658—dc22

                                                    2008026400

Printing number

10 9 8 7 6

THE NEW MANAGER'S TOOL KIT

To our clients:
past, present, and future…
and to all who share our vision:
Organizational success in perfect accord
with individual fulfillment.

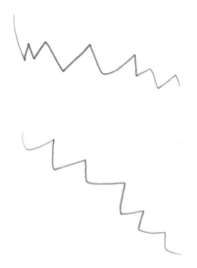

CONTENTS

PREFACE xi

INTRODUCTION:
A Tool Kit for Today's Workplace, 1

PART ONE:
Leading People, 6

What Do Employees Want?, 6

TOOL #1:
Turn On Talent … and Turn Off Turnover, 9

TOOL #2:
Unleash Their Productivity, 25

TOOL #3:
Balance Their Work and Life, 33

PART TWO:
Different Strokes, 38

Individual Differences, 38

TOOL #4:
Embrace Diversity, 41

TOOL #5:
Get a Grip on Generations, 57

TOOL #6:
Focus On Ability, 65

PART THREE:
Leader Effectiveness, 78

Open Two-Way Communication, 78

TOOL #7:
Tell Them What Worked ... and What Didn't, 81

TOOL #8:
Ask Them ... Then Listen, 89

PART FOUR:
Optimizing Contributions, 96

The Three Strategies ... and a Precursor, 96

TOOL #9:
Diagnose Problems, 99

TOOL #10:

Coach the Good Ones ... and the Not So Good, 103

TOOL #11:

Mentor the Great Ones, 110

TOOL #12:

Turn On Teamwork, 114

PART FIVE:

Personal and Interpersonal Effectiveness, 120

Life Skills, 120

TOOL #13:

Blow Away Burnout, 123

TOOL #14:

Stay on Top of Stress, 133

TOOL #15:

Accentuate the Positive, 139

TOOL #16:

Assert Yourself ... and Deal with "Difficult" People, 151

TOOL #17:

Own Your Anger ... Don't Let It Own You, 161

TOOL #18:

Rise to the Challenge of Change, 172

6
PART SIX:
Eliminating Conflict, 178

Barriers to an Effective Workplace, 178

TOOL #19:
Prevent All Forms of Harassment, 181

TOOL #20:
Prevent Workplace Violence, 197

TOOL #21:
Defuse and Protect, 214

Afterword, 222

APPENDIX A:
Ten Tips to Protect Against Harassment Charges, 223

APPENDIX B:
Ten Steps to Manage Workplace Violence, 227

APPENDIX C:
The Impending Leadership Crisis, 232

Resource Guide—Books and Websites Organized by Tool, 239

INDEX 251

PREFACE

THE NEW MANAGER

This book is intended for "new" managers (of any job title). That certainly includes first-time managers (as well as those preparing for that role). And it also includes experienced managers (at all levels) who feel a need for a fresh approach to the challenges of leading people in today's workplace.

If you are a first-time manager, we suspect that you were quite competent as an individual contributor, which is why you were chosen for your current role. However, you may not be feeling that same level of competence in your new position, yet. You're facing a very different set of challenges. Chief among them is getting things done through *others*. This book will guide you on your journey.

If you are an experienced manager, you may be reeling from a dizzying array of new challenges—a rapidly changing (even dangerous) marketplace and workplace, increasing legal restrictions, a shrinking (but more demanding and different) workforce, and a global 24/7 world. This book will help you find your way through the maze.

MANAGER VS. LEADER

Many books distinguish between these two terms, stating that management is about authority, whereas leadership is about influence. We don't. In today's workplace, anyone with management responsibilities must use *leadership* to execute those responsibilities. Most of today's employees will not tolerate an authoritarian style. And even those few who might put up with being ordered around will be less effective under such a taskmaster.

Also, the term *manager* includes both managing tasks and managing people. This is a book about managing people, in other words, *leadership*.

We use these two terms almost interchangeably, primarily using *manager* or *management* to refer to the job responsibility; *leader* as a generic term for various job titles; and *leadership* to refer to the means of executing that responsibility when dealing with people.

ACKNOWLEDGMENTS

When we began writing this book, we had no idea of the extent to which others would make invaluable direct or indirect contributions. They include Peter Schwartz, Pearl Goodman, Tal Etstein, Leslie Charles, Ralph Parilla, Bob Nelson, Larry Chavez, Carol-Susan DeVaney, Dwight McKay, Dr. Gayle Carson, and Dr. Peter Dana; the individuals and organizations referenced throughout the book; our agent Bill Gladstone at Waterside Productions; our editor Christina Parisi at AMACOM; our newsletter readers; and the participants in our workshops and presentations.

Without their support or insight, this book would never have seen the light of day nor possessed many of the positive qualities it may have. Thank you all!

THE NEW MANAGER'S TOOL KIT

A Tool Kit for Today's Workplace

─┤ MANAGING PEOPLE ├─

The single greatest challenge in today's workplace is the management of that most inscrutable of resources—people.

All too often, organizations view their employees in much the same way as they view their material resources: as a commodity, homogeneous and easily interchangeable. For example, notice the frequent use of such terms as *human capital, subordinate, rank and file*, and *headcount*—terms that connote property, servitude, or thingness.

In fact, however, employees are not headcount, nor merely the means to organizational ends. They are also ends unto themselves. As a *human* resource, an employee deserves (and needs) to be viewed differently than the inanimate resources of the organization. A human being needs to be treated with *respect*. The power tool to tap the full potential of your workplace is grasping this fact, not only intellectually but also in your gut, so that it influences every aspect of how you think about and interact with this invaluable "asset"—your fellow employees.

The various ramifications of this power tool are the 21 tools in this book. They provide a fresh approach to employee management in today's diverse, globally competitive, 24/7 world—informed by new paradigms and recent studies. The tools unlock:

1. Classic managerial challenges: coaching, mentoring, and motivating employees, optimizing performance, teamwork, and two-way communication.

2. Fundamental personal and interpersonal skills: attitude, assertion, dealing with "difficult" people, and managing stress and anger.

3. Issues of special relevance to today's workplace: employee retention, work/life balance, diversity, multiple generations at work, disabilities, rapid change, job burnout, harassment, and workplace violence.

Anyone who regularly uses the power tool, and each of the 21 tools as they are needed, will, indeed, *hit the ground running*.

RESPECT

Most of us, perhaps, share a similar understanding of the word *respect*. But the concept of respect is so important, and so essential to this book, that we are elaborating on it.

The *American Heritage Dictionary* defines respect as "the state of being regarded with honor or esteem." As a verb, the definition includes "to avoid violation of."

This second definition provides an important clarification. By respect, we do not mean deference to authority or position (e.g., bowing to a king or "Yes sir, boss!"). Rather, we are referring to the American principle of avoiding violation of an individual's fundamental rights. Every human being is a sir or ma'am, even when you address them on an informal, first-name basis.

And we've created an acronym based on the word *respect*, which enumerates some of the behaviors associated with it:

Refrain from put-downs, criticism, personal attacks.

Encourage others to state their views.

Support each other, even if you don't agree.

Practice active listening.

Express yourself assertively, not aggressively or submissively.

Collaborate, do not compete or collude.

Trust each other, unless and until such trust is violated.

In our training programs, we ask participants to commit to these behaviors. We urge you to do likewise in your workplace.

WORKPLACE LEADERS

According to a recent 10-year study conducted by Rainmaker Thinking, Inc. (based on interviews with over 10,000 employees and executives at more than 700 different organizations):

> The day-to-day communication between supervisory managers and direct reports has more impact than any other single factor on employee productivity, quality, morale, and retention.
>
> **Immediate supervisors are now the most important people in the workplace.**

This applies to "immediate supervisors" of any job title and at every level of an organization, from first-line team leaders to senior executives, that is, leaders. This book is for them, and for those preparing to move into leadership roles.

We define *leader* as a person who guides and influences people to willingly follow a chosen direction.

Leadership requires:

1. Having a clear and consistent vision and mission (i.e., the chosen direction), communicated effectively
2. Guiding people toward the vision, to be effective in accomplishing the mission
3. Influencing people to willingly follow that direction

The New Manager's Tool Kit shows you how to do this.

WHO CAN BENEFIT FROM THIS BOOK

Obvious beneficiaries are current workplace leaders, that is, those individuals whose job responsibilities include (in whole or in part) the work of others:

- At every level and in any function of an organization
- With any given amount of experience

*   In organizations of any size and in every economic sector

We have found that the issues are essentially the same, regardless, not only for those already in leadership positions but also for those preparing for leadership roles, both the currently employed and students.

In addition, this book will be of interest to those working in job functions that specialize in the topics addressed, such as human resources (HR), training, security, safety, and employee assistance programs (EAP).

─┤   HOW TO USE THIS BOOK   ├─

The New Manager's Tool Kit is both a how-to and why-to book. The 21 tools address principles and techniques, skills to implement those techniques, skills for personal and interpersonal effectiveness, and barriers to an effective workplace.

Each tool explores a hot topic. We describe the nature of the topic and why it is hot (i.e., especially relevant to today's workplace), referencing current data, studies, and headlines. Many of the topics (e.g., motivation, stress, work/life, diversity, etc.) are commonly regarded as nice-to-do's or should-do's. We also point out each topic's impact on the bottom line.

You will discover the underlying **Secret** to each tool (the essential concept, often from a unique perspective), learn practical tips to implement the secret (with detailed examples, scenarios, or practice activities), and begin applications for your workplace.

You may read this book from cover to cover for a comprehensive exploration of how to lead people in today's workplace. A new or prospective leader or a student might choose this approach and will find the book organized in a meaningful way.

Current leaders with some experience may want to go directly to specific sections or tools that interest them. So, for example, if you've just experienced an incident of workplace violence, don't hesitate to proceed to Tool #20. This approach works very well. Many of the tools are self-standing and we provide references to other relevant tools and to additional resources, as needed. (In addition, see the Resource Guide.)

All of the tools are derived from the training programs we have developed and conducted during the past 10 years in response to the requests by clients for our training and speaking services.

——[**HOW THIS BOOK IS ORGANIZED**]——

The 21 tools in *The New Manager's Tool Kit* are organized into six parts:

Part 1. Leading People provides the foundation for influencing today's employees and deals with such topics as motivating and energizing them, reducing turnover, enhancing productivity, and balancing work/life.

Part 2. Different Strokes fine-tunes these insights to acknowledge differences among employees, such as abilities and personality, but concentrates on three issues of special relevance in today's workplace: diversity, four generations at work, and employees with disabilities.

Part 3. Leader Effectiveness teaches the communication skills leaders need to influence or guide. You will learn how to provide positive and constructive feedback, inquire, and listen.

Part 4. Optimizing Contributions unlocks the application of the skills in Part 3 and other skills to guide employees by diagnosing performance problems, coaching marginal and good employees, mentoring the great ones, and building teams.

Part 5. Personal and Interpersonal Effectiveness teaches additional skills needed by leaders to interact with others in the workplace and to deal with life challenges in general. You will learn how to alleviate job burnout, stay on top of stress, maintain a positive attitude, become more assertive, deal with difficult people, manage anger, and rise to the challenge of change.

Part 6. Eliminating Conflict addresses two of the most significant barriers to an effective workplace—harassment and violence.

We also provide a resource guide to explore any of these issues in greater depth, as well as appendices with tools relevant to workplace leadership, but not of immediate concern to first-line managers—policies and procedures for protecting against harassment charges and managing violence, and suggestions to prepare for an impending leadership crisis.

1

Leading People

WHAT DO EMPLOYEES WANT?

What do you think employees most want from their jobs? Good wages? Job security? That's what most managers have thought for at least the past 60 years.

But it is not what employees continue to say! As shown in Table 1-1, what employees really want are appreciation and involvement.

Note the glaring disconnect between manager opinion and employee fact.

Are we saying—or are employees saying—that competitive wages are unimportant? Of course not. Money usually is a necessary but not a sufficient condition to attract, retain, and motivate good employees. (By the way, money isn't even always necessary. Notice how energized and enthusiastic unpaid volunteers often are.)

Test this out yourself. Remember a time when you felt energized, fulfilled, and excited about your job or a project, when you couldn't wait to get out of bed and get to work. If, unfortunately, nothing comes to mind, remember a time when you felt frustrated, bored, or dispirited about your job, when you had to force yourself out of bed to go to work.

What were you doing and what was special—or *not* special—about it? Was it the pay and fringe benefits? Maybe, for the first few days. Or was it the stimulating work, the stretching of your abilities, being an important part of a grand venture, the rapport with coworkers, the recognition from superiors?

Table 1-1. What Employees Want from Their Jobs

Factors	Managers	Employees
Full Appreciation for Work Done	8	(1)
Good Wages	(1)	5
Good Working Conditions	4	9
Interesting Work	5	6
Job Security	(2)	4
Promotion/Growth Opportunities	(3)	7
Personal Loyalty to Workers	6	8
Feeling "In" on Things	10	(2)
Sympathetic Help on Personal Problems	9	(3)
Tactful Disciplining	7	10

SOURCES: Foreman Facts, Labor Relations Institute of New York (1946); Lawrence Lindahl, *Personnel Magazine* (1949)

Repeated with similar results: Ken Kovach (1980); Valerie Wilson, Achievers International (1988); Bob Nelson, Blanchard Training & Development (1991); Sheryl & Don Grimme, GHR Training Solutions (1997–Present)

If you find that it's the former, please write to us. (You'll be the first; and we have been asking this same question for years—on our websites and in our newsletter, workshops, and presentations.) Otherwise, the only thing we would add to your insight is the assurance that such insight is not unique—to you, your profession, job level, generation, or socioeconomic group.

And notice that while managers rank promotion/growth opportunities among the top three motivators, employees rank this toward the bottom. This is important to some employees (perhaps to you), but overall, not so much.

Lest there be any doubt, these discrepancies between manager opinion and employee fact are *good* news, for at least two reasons. First, increased wages and job security (which managers think are most important) are precisely what many organizations cannot provide these days; whereas appreciation and involvement, which employees really want, can be provided anytime, at little or no cost. As for those promotion and growth opportunities, often you are not able to provide these to many of your employees. The second reason is that most managers out there don't really get it. If you do, your department and organization can win the battle for leading people, regardless of budget.

This is all very nice, but you are trying to run an enterprise. How does this affect the bottom line?

Well, in 1998, The Gallup Organization studied the impact of employee attitudes on business outcomes. They found that organizations—where employees have above average attitudes toward their work—have:

- 38 percent higher customer satisfaction scores
- 22 percent higher productivity
- 22 percent better employee retention
- 27 percent higher profits

Satisfying employees is not only a nice thing to do, it also makes good business sense.

Our first tool unlocks employee retention with a deeper exploration of motivation. We examine the current challenge of retention, review some classic motivation theories, introduce our own 3-Factor Theory, present hard data from recent landmark studies that support the theories, reveal the secret and our Top 10 Tips to turn on talent and turn off turnover, and launch you on an application to apply all of this to your staff.

Tool #2 releases employee productivity by exposing a phenomenon that is impairing it—increased job demands. We examine that phenomenon, including highlights from recent studies, share our secret for dealing with it, provide tips to ameliorate the negative impact of job demands, and suggest an initial application for your workplace.

Tool #3 opens an issue of increasing importance to today's employees: work/life balance. You will learn how important it really is, the critical role you play, the secret, and specific principles to deal with it effectively. As always, an application is included.

TOOL ONE

Turn On Talent ... and Turn Off Turnover

There is a crisis in America today. The one we're talking about has nothing to do with telemarketing, as annoying as that is, or even the troubling economy. Rather, we're referring to the diminishing ability of organizations in every sector of our society to attract, retain, and motivate talented employees, that is, to survive.

It is employee retention especially that has emerged as the workplace issue of the decade. In 2006, the Society for Human Resource Management (SHRM), in its Workplace Forecast, predicted that the number one employment trend most likely to have a major impact on the workplace is a greater emphasis on retention strategies.

And in a 2007 study by the global employee retention research firm TalentKeepers, 88 percent of employers reported turnover had stayed the same or increased...and 45 percent forecasted a further increase in turnover (only 3 percent predicted a decrease).

You see, our long-held assumption of an ever-expanding talent pool has been shattered by such factors as the retirement of aging Baby Boomers, lower birthrates, tighter immigration rules, and an increase in the skills demanded for today's jobs.

The first three factors explain this quantitatively. But it is the last one, the qualitative factor, that is the sticking point. More than a shortage of bodies, this is a crisis of abilities—the talent in "talent pool."

In addition, employee loyalty is down. According to a 2005 survey conducted by the Society for Human Resource Management, 79 percent of employees are job searching, either actively or passively. In fact, the most frequently asked question put to SHRM is, "How can we keep talent from jumping to our competitors?"

Fortunately, every crisis contains not only danger but also opportunity. In this tool, you will learn the secret to transforming this dangerous crisis into an opportunity for you and your organization to flourish.

TRANSFORMING DANGER INTO OPPORTUNITY

Employers are groping for ways to attack the problem. The 2005 SHRM survey found that the techniques used are salary adjustments, job promotions, bonuses, more attractive benefits and retirement packages, and stock options—all of which are expensive and (as found in the 2007 TalentKeepers' study) not very effective. The reason, as you will see, is that they are misdirected.

Rather than leaping to implement techniques, it is important to begin with an understanding of what really energizes and instills loyalty in employees. Otherwise, you won't know whether any technique is effective and you won't be very effective in implementing it.

UNDERSTANDING HUMAN MOTIVATION—THEORY

The best known motivation theory is probably Maslow's Hierarchy of Needs, shown in Figure 1-1.

Maslow categorized human needs into five sets:

1. The most fundamental is *survival.* This is our need for food, water, and shelter, and in the modern era includes medical services, electricity, transportation, and phones, all of which

Figure 1-1. Maslow's Hierarchy of Needs.

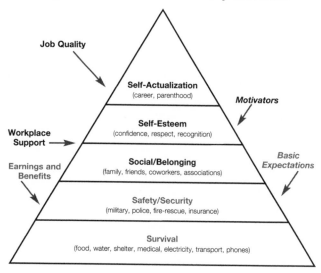

are jeopardized by natural disasters. Visualize the aftermath of Hurricane Katrina.

2. Next is *safety/security* for which we look to the military, police, fire-rescue, and insurance. All of these were called into play on and since 9/11.

3. What then emerges is *social/belonging*—our need for family, friends, coworkers, and associations.

4. Then comes *self-esteem*—confidence, respect, appreciation, and recognition.

5. And the ultimate is *self-actualization*—fulfillment and happiness, which most of us meet through career, marriage, and/or parenthood.

Maslow did more than just categorize. He posited that these needs do not have equal force all the time. When our fundamental needs of survival, safety, and security are threatened, say, by hurricanes or terrorism, that's all we care about. As South Florida residents, we have firsthand knowledge of this. For the first several days after Hurricane Wilma in 2005, local television stations had no network programming, not even national news. All they reported was where to get water and ice, and where and when power was being restored.

However, for most Americans most of the time, these needs are met. They become merely basic expectations (what psychologist Frederick Herzberg called "hygiene" factors) that we pay little attention to. What we care about and are motivated by are the three highest-level needs.

Maslow's hierarchy provides a springboard for our own 3-Factor Theory (Figure 1-2), which consolidates two other theories (Herzberg's 2-Factor Theory and the Kano Model of Customer Satisfaction) from an employer's perspective.

As notated in Figure 1-1, employers satisfy Maslow's fundamental survival, safety, and security needs primarily through a paycheck and benefits plan: *Earnings and Benefits*. This is how employees buy groceries, put a roof over their heads, and insure against life's contingencies.

In the workplace, the highest-level need of self-actualization and much of our self-esteem are met through the work itself: *Job Quality*.

Employers can address the center rung of social and belonging needs, as well as self-esteem, with *Workplace Support*, for example, supervision, teamwork, and recognition.

As Figure 1-2 shows, each of these three sets of factors is different in nature and effect. (You can get a free, online audiovisual tutorial on the Kano Model of Customer Satisfaction, upon which Figure 1-2 is based, by visiting the site of C2C Solutions. It's brief and easy to understand.)

As Herzberg maintained, the absence of Earnings and Benefits is demotivating. These are what Kano calls *basic needs*. If a job's pay and benefits are inadequate to pay our bills, we won't even start work. If we feel unfairly compensated, we will gripe and complain. But we're not really motivated by overpay or lavish benefits. That's not to say we won't enjoy them, but they are not truly energizing.

In contrast, the very presence of Job Quality is motivating—Kano's *excitement needs*. The greater our sense of achievement and the more involved we are in our work, the more energized and excited we become. This really turns us on!

We maintain that the Workplace Support factors are both demotivators *and* motivators—Kano's *performance needs*. A lousy supervisor, coworker friction, and lack of appreciation drains our energy. But the better our supervisor is, the more cohesive our team, and the more appreciated we feel, the more energized we become.

Figure 1-2. Grimme's 3-Factor Theory.

Put another way, we will go to work for a paycheck and a benefits plan. But we won't really do work (or, at least, our best work) unless something else is present. It is the quality of the work itself and of our relationships with others at work that draws us to the best organizations and keeps us there, energized and performing at peak effectiveness.

Well, all that is just theory. Here now is…

⎯⎯⎯⎯⏐ DATA THAT SUPPORTS THE THEORY ⏐⎯⎯⎯⎯

Every five years, the Families and Work Institute conducts its National Study of the Changing Workforce. It is, perhaps, the most comprehensive research ever conducted on the American workplace. Each time, the focus is a bit different.

In 1997, the National Study examined the impact on work outcomes of four sets of factors: Earnings and Benefits, Job Quality, Workplace Support, and Job Demands. (You can see where the labels for our 3-Factor Theory originated.)

The National Study found that while earnings and benefits have only a 2 percent impact on job satisfaction, job quality and workplace support

Figure 1-3. Factors Impacting Job Satisfaction.

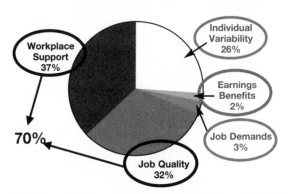

Job Quality	Workplace Support	Earnings and Benefits	Job Demands
Job autonomy	Flexibility	Pay	Hours worked
Learning opportunities	Supervisor support	Traditional benefits	Nights away from home
Meaningfulness of job	Workplace culture	Dependent-care benefits	Overtime with no notice
Advancement opportunities	Coworker relations		Shift work
Job security	Equal opportunity		Job pressures
	Lack of discrimination		
	Respect		

Derived from *The 1997 National Study of the Changing Workforce,* Families and Work Institute, No. 2, 1997.

have a combined 70 percent impact. That's a 35 times greater bang for the buck! Although in the case of job quality and workplace support, it's a symbolic buck rather than a monetary expense.

The results were similar for factors impacting organizational loyalty, employee retention, and job performance. (For job performance, there was another factor that also emerged, which we discuss in the next tool.)

──┤ APPLYING THE THEORY AND THE DATA ├──

As a workplace leader, you can put this 3-Factor Theory and data to *practical* use.

These concepts can become your mental model or paradigm, guiding you as you interact with your employees on a day-to-day and minute-by-minute basis. It is a very different paradigm from the carrot-and-stick approach typically used and is much more effective in getting the bottom-line results you want.

You can think about your own behaviors and your organization's current policies, practices, and programs from what may be a different perspective. Are they working for you? Are they consistent with these principles? What changes can you begin to make?

You can anticipate the efficacy of new initiatives under consideration. For example, to reduce turnover, does it now make sense to rely on salary increases, promotions, bonuses, benefits, retirement packages, and stock options?

You can think about the following secret—and the secrets of all 21 tools in this book—in light of this theory and paradigm. And as you apply each tool's tips, you will likely be more effective because you will have a greater understanding and belief in them.

THE *SECRET* TO MOTIVATING AND RETAINING TALENTED EMPLOYEES

By now, the **Secret** we promised you may be obvious. In a nutshell:

1. Pay them fairly.
2. **Treat them *GREAT!***

As for how to treat them great, we developed...

GRIMME'S TOP 10 TIPS TO MOTIVATE AND RETAIN TALENTED EMPLOYEES

As you read these tips, we'd like you to think about this tool's application—what *you* can begin doing as a leader. Included with the tips are real-world examples (many of which are taken from Bob Nelson's *1001 Ways to Reward Employees* and *1001 Ways to Energize Employees*). The employers in the examples may be larger or smaller or in a different industry or sector than your organization. Think about how you can *adapt* the ideas to your workplace.

Tip #1: Pay *employees fairly and well; then* get them to forget *about money.*

This tip has two parts. The importance of the first part is illuminated by Equity Theory, the highlights of which are shown in Figure 1-4.

Figure 1-4. Equity Theory.

- Employees compare their **own** outcomes/inputs with *others*:

$$\frac{\textbf{Own } \text{Outcomes}}{\textbf{Own } \text{Inputs}} \quad \overset{?}{=} \quad \frac{\textit{Others'} \text{ Outcomes}}{\textit{Others'} \text{ Inputs}}$$

- If employees perceive **in**equity, they will act to **correct** it:
  - Lower Productivity
  - Increased Absenteeism
  - Reduced Quality
  - Increased Turnover

What Equity Theory basically says is that if employees believe they are unfairly paid, they will be demotivated. They will complain, goof off, and eventually quit. And, in fact, most employees (not necessarily yours) do not believe they are paid fairly. But assuming that wages are competitive and fair, studies have shown that pay itself has no impact on retention or productivity. In fact, focusing on pay may actually denigrate performance.

Therefore, the second part of our tip is to then get them to forget about money. Don't bother coming up with a complicated incentive pay program, particularly if it pits employees against one another. Such programs just get in the way of employees focusing their attention where it should be—on doing a good job!

Tip #2: Treat each and every employee with respect. Show *that you care about each employee as a* person, *not just as a worker.*

If you have not yet read the Introduction to this book (about respect), now would be a good time to do so.

Beth Israel Hospital is one employer that has established an interesting method of ensuring that all its employees are treated with respect.

At Beth Israel Hospital in Boston, Massachusetts, doctors occasionally dress as maintenance staff and roam the hospital halls. Why do they do that? To learn how it feels to be treated as "support staff" and to find ways of improving the hospital environment.

In another instance, to show employees that it cares about them as persons:

Publix supermarkets publishes a biweekly bulletin that lists the births, deaths, marriages, and illnesses of employees and their families. For more than 20 years, the president sent personalized cards to the families of everyone in the bulletin.

By the way, Publix is considered one of the 100 best companies to work for.

Notice in that ongoing 60-year study in Table 1-1, one of the things employees most want is Sympathetic Help on Personal Problems. The phrasing of this factor was more in vogue back in the 1940s, when that study began. Today, this probably would be called something like Sensitivity to Work/Life Issues. It's even more significant to today's employees.

And studies show that more important than flextime, telecommuting, or onsite day care, simple respect is considered the number one need for balancing work/life issues. We will say more about work/life balance in Tool #3. For now, here's an impressive example:

When Steve Peterson's three-year-old son had open-heart surgery and his wife was confined to bed with a high-risk pregnancy, his employer, Hewitt Associates, arranged for him to work part-time for three months, maintained his benefits, and installed a computer at his home so he could be with his family.

How loyal and committed to his employer do you think Steve has been since then?

Tip #3: Praise *accomplishments...and attempts.*

Praise accomplishments using positive feedback, a skill you will learn in Tool #7. Remember, more than anything else, employees want to be appreciated for the work they do.

And not only accomplishments but also good attempts, just as you would if you were training a puppy or a young child. We are not suggesting that employees are pets or children, but the principle applies to any living organism.

Praise accomplishments both large and small. Here is an example of a small reward for a large accomplishment:

> A Hewlett-Packard engineer burst into his manager's office to announce he had just found the solution to a problem the group had been struggling with for many weeks. His manager quickly groped around his desk for some item to acknowledge the accomplishment and ended up handing the employee a banana from his lunch with the words, "Well done. Congratulations!" The employee was initially puzzled, but over time, the Golden Banana Award became one of the most prestigious honors bestowed on an inventive employee.

A reward can have little or no monetary value and still be effective. It's the meaning attached to the reward that counts.

Praise at least four times more than you criticize, which, for many of us, is in the reverse proportion to what we tend to receive. (We say more about criticizing in the next tip.)

Do it promptly, as soon as observed. Praise delayed is praise denied. Do not wait for the annual performance review. Remember the puppy/child principle.

Do it verbally and in writing. Putting praise in writing does not have to be time-consuming. For example, use your business card. When you catch someone doing something right, briefly note what the person did and how you feel about it. Sign it and hand the person the card.

Dear Reader,

Congratulations for caring about motivating your employees!

Well Done!

Don & Sheryl Grimme

Do it publicly and in private (as we just did) based on both the magnitude of the accomplishment and the personal preferences of the recipient. Not everyone is comfortable with public praise.

And do it sincerely. For example, if right after we praised you we asked you to use our training services, would you feel appreciated…or manipulated?

An interesting study was conducted a few years back on the impact of appreciation practices.

Figure 1-5. Impact of 28 Appreciation Practices.

The Four Most Effective	The Four Least Effective
1. Personal thanks	25. Employee of the Month
2. Written thanks	26. Gifts or parties on birthday
3. Promotion for performance	27. Birthday cards
4. Public praise	28. Hats, t-shirts with company logo

SOURCE: Dr. Gerald Graham, Wichita State University, 1990

Notice the four most effective appreciation practices. What do these have in common? They are specific, personalized, and based on actual performance.

Now look at the four least effective. These tend to be generalized, impersonal, or unrelated to performance. Ironically, they are also the most common. For example, what workplace doesn't have an Employee of the Month program or birthday parties? **Note:** Although hats and t-shirts with the organization's logo have little to do with appreciation, they can be valuable for team building. As for birthday parties, see Tip #10.

Tip #4: Clearly communicate goals, responsibilities, and expectations. Never criticize in public—redirect in private.

Just as we have our Top 10 Tips to Motivate Employees, Dean Spitzer came up with the Top 10 Ways to *Zap* Employee Motivation. They include unclear expectations, withholding information, and criticism.

You can implement this tip by using something called *constructive feedback*, the second skill you will learn in Tool #7. As you will see, constructive feedback *clarifies* expectations, *provides* information, and, when done right, is *not* criticism (even in private).

Tip #5: *Recognize performance* appropriately and consistently.

On the one hand, reward outstanding performance, for example, with promotions and opportunities. But don't do it just with big rewards like these. A metaphor for rewards is a nurse giving a lollipop to a patient. Applying this metaphor to employee rewards is not quite as silly as you might think.

> Sam Colin, founder of a janitorial services company, used to go around handing out Life Savers candy to employees. That early tradition developed into a lasting philosophy of recognition, which includes such awards as Most Helpful and Nicest Employee...as voted on by coworkers.

This may sound like those Employee of the Month awards we just said were not that effective. However, notice that these awards are voted on by coworkers. Having the employees themselves determine the results gets them involved, and it minimizes their resentment of the award recipients.

On the other hand, do not tolerate sustained poor performance. Instead, provide coaching and training (see Tool #10). If that doesn't work, fire the person! This may sound obvious, but studies show that most employees do not believe that poor performers are dealt with effectively.

Tip #6: *Involve employees in plans and decisions,* especially those that affect them. Solicit *employees' ideas and opinions. Encourage* initiative.

The Dilbert cartoons are known for their humorous commentary on the dysfunctional workplace. An ongoing theme of the series is plans and decisions handed down from on high in which the employees had no input and that (unsurprisingly) are impossible to implement.

Recall from the 60-year study cited at the beginning of this section that employees want to feel they are in on things. Do *your* employees feel in on things? They can if you solicit their ideas and opinions, using the inquiry skill in Tool #8.

When developing new training courses, many corporate universities interview and poll their target audience to determine their most pressing needs and learning style preferences. How relevant and popular do you think the resulting training programs are likely to be?

And encourage initiative. All too often, employees who rock the boat or stick their necks out by expressing creative ideas are slapped down rather than rewarded. Recognizing this...

The CEO of Hershey Foods created a special award he called The Exalted Order of the Extended Neck "to reward people who were willing to buck the system, practice a little entrepreneurship, and were willing to stand the heat for an idea they really believed in."

Tip #7: Create opportunities for employees to learn and grow. Link the goals of the organization with the goals of each individual in it.

You may wonder why learn and grow is a Top 10 Tip. After all, according to that ongoing 60-year study, most employees are lukewarm about promotion/growth opportunities.

Well, the National Study of the Changing Workforce also examined how employees choose employers (Figure 1-6).

Figure 1-6. How Employees Choose Employers.

1. Open communications	9. Coworker quality
2. Effect on personal/family life	10. Stimulating work
3. Nature of work	11. Job location
4. Management quality	12. Family-supportive policies
5. Supervisor	13. Fringe benefits
6. Gain new skills ←	14. Control of work schedule
7. Control over work content →	15. *Advancement opportunity*
8. Job security	16. Salary/wage

SOURCE: *The Changing Workforce: Highlights of the (1992) National Study,* Families and Work Institute, 1993.

Of the 16 factors studied, advancement opportunity was ranked near the bottom, but gaining new skills ranked toward the top. Some of your employees want to climb the organizational ladder. Virtually all of your employees want to learn and grow. This certainly includes formal education and training programs, as well as informal on-the-job training.

Consider also implementing a Job-for-a-Day program, where each employee assists an employee in another department to perform his or her job. They will gain a greater perspective of your enterprise as a whole and esprit de corps will be enhanced.

Whether to gain new skills or to advance, employees probably will need to change jobs or departments from time to time. To facilitate this, many organizations utilize internal job posting systems. The better systems:

- Post all job openings (other than entry level)
- Give consideration to internal candidates prior to external candidates
- Require that all qualified candidates be interviewed
- Provide feedback to all those not selected indicating why not

Link the goals of the organization with the goals of each individual in it. All employees should be clear about how the work they do contributes to your organization's mission and to themselves. We say more about making this linkage in the next tool.

Tip #8: Actively listen to employees' concerns—both work-related and personal.

You'll learn about the active listening skill in Tool #8. Here are two examples:

> Once a month, a manager at the Mirage Hotel in Las Vegas, Nevada, asks her staff, "What one thing can I do better for you?" After listening to and acknowledging the employees' ideas, she tells them one thing they can do better for her.

That's what one manager can do. This is what an entire corporation has done:

> Motorola's Individual Dignity Entitlement Program requires managers and supervisors to meet one-on-one with each member of their staff every three months. They discuss employees' answers to six questions about how they are treated. Then action plans to address issues are created and the progress toward previous action plans is reviewed.

Tip #9: Share information—promptly, openly, and clearly. Tell the truth...with compassion.

Take a second look at that 1992 National Study referenced earlier and notice what is *most* important to prospective employees.

Figure 1-7. How Employees Choose Employers.

1. **Open communications**	9. Coworker quality
2. Effect on personal/family life	10. Stimulating work
3. Nature of work	11. Job location
4. Management quality	12. Family-supportive policies
5. Supervisor	13. Fringe benefits
6. Gain new skills	14. Control of work schedule
7. Control over work content	15. Advancement opportunity
8. Job security	16. Salary/wage

SOURCE: *The Changing Workforce: Highlights of the (1992) National Study,* Families and Work Institute, 1993.

How do your employees find out what's really going on? Via the rumor mill? Or from effective and trusted communication programs? And you can empower them in the process. For example, at many manufacturing companies, each product line tracks its own quality and productivity, posting the results for all to see.

Tell the truth...with compassion. If layoffs or benefits cuts are in the works, let your employees know and help them deal with it.

The executives at each Motorola facility hold quarterly Town Hall Meetings with all employees to communicate business results and plans and to respond to employee questions and concerns.

Tip #10: Celebrate *successes and milestones reached—both organizational and personal.* Create an organizational culture that is open, trusting, and fun.

The Publix Super Markets' bulletin of births and marriages is an example of personal milestones. Here are examples that combine both organizational and personal milestones.

The signatures of all 48 employees who worked on the first Macintosh computer (not just Jobs and Wozniak) were molded on the inside of the product's case. Imagine the pride those employees felt then...and today.

Verizon Wireless named cell sites after top employees. Think about how you could adapt such practices to your products, services, and work environment.

Create an organizational culture that is open, trusting, and fun.

On his first day at Hewitt Associates, a new hire received a welcome note and a "survival kit" (including a candy bar and nerf ball). Everyone came by his office to personally welcome him to the team. Then, every day for the next two weeks, someone made a point to stop by and ask him to lunch.

Do you think that new employee felt a sense of belonging at Hewitt? And for pure fun:

The employees at Miami's Baptist Hospital give themselves a break by throwing a Monotony Breaker Day on minor holidays (e.g., Oktoberfest). Employees are encouraged to drop by the party room whenever convenient to socialize or just relax and take a break.

APPLICATION

1. What *people challenges* are you facing at your workplace? For example:
   * Turnover, absenteeism, lateness
   * Morale, esprit de corps
   * Productivity, commitment

2. *Visualize* your staff as a whole and each person in it.

3. *Ask yourself:* What are their needs? Frustrations?
   * Recognition, appreciation, fair rewards
   * Development of skills, career, personal
   * Meaningful work/feeling involved
   * Respected and listened to
   * Receive clear feedback and information
   * Celebrate successes/have fun

4. Not sure? Ask *them.*

5. Prepare a *plan of action* and *execute* it—starting now!

Unleash Their Productivity

In 2006, we were quoted in a Reuters' news story entitled "Americans Work More, Seem to Accomplish Less." The story's premise was that technology, instead of improving productivity, is interfering with it.

Actually, we don't agree with this premise. There is no question in our minds that technology (e.g., personal computers, e-mail, the Internet) has dramatically improved productivity.

It may seem like many of us are accomplishing less. However, it has more to do with expectations than technology. Even if productivity increases, it is constantly outpaced by those expectations. The irony is that the very expectation of getting more done is getting in the way of getting more done. People are stressed out.

A 2005 in-depth study by the Families and Work Institute found that one-third of all U.S. employees are chronically overworked.

Downsizing, global competition, 24/7 operations, and dual careers have enhanced the products and services we can purchase as consumers. However, these same factors have increased the demands placed on us as producers, that is, in the workplace. And many of us, as individuals and as organizations, have not yet adjusted to this brave new world.

In addition to the study previously referenced, every five years the Families and Work Institute conducts the National Study of the Changing

Workforce. In 1997, the National Study examined the impact on work outcomes of four factors.

In Tool #1, we brought to your attention the two factors having the greatest impact on job satisfaction, employee loyalty, and retention: Job Quality and Workplace Support.

For job performance (productivity), however, another factor emerges: Job Demands. These are stress factors, like long hours and job pressures, which exhaust us and drain our emotional reserves.

Job Demands

    Hours worked

    Bringing work home

    Nights away from home

    Overtime with no notice

    Shift work

    Job pressures

As shown in the Figure 2-1 pie chart, such Job Demands have a significant impact on performance, a *negative* one—comparable to the *positive* impact of either Job Quality or Workplace Support.

This is not good news. This first decade of the new millennium is the era of working smarter *and* harder, 24/7. The very standards that demand high performance are having a negative impact on that performance.

So what to do? Well, you can start by doing whatever you can to limit these job demands. Be sure to include job burnout in your equation when assessing the relative merits of cost-cutting or productivity improvement initiatives. (See Tool #13 for what individuals can do to alleviate their own burnout.)

Think about what you can do to limit each type of job demand listed above:

- Discourage excessively long hours and bringing work home, whenever possible.
- Minimize nights away from home (for example, use virtual meetings).
- Limit overtime (which is a good way to cut costs) and plan for it in advance.

Figure 2-1. *1997 National Study of the Changing Workforce.*
Factors Impacting Job Performance.

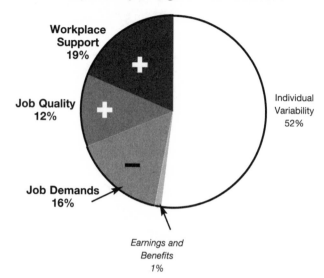

- Accommodate personal preferences in shift assignments, whenever possible.
- Make sure that your productivity expectations are reasonable.
- Use motivation, rather than pressure, to encourage your employees to meet those expectations.

And there is some good news! The National Study also found that workplace support appears to buffer or protect employees from the negative effects of job demands.

Our **Secret,** therefore, is to...

Beef up workplace support to ameliorate the negative
impact of job demands on productivity.

To unleash the productivity of your employees, place a renewed emphasis on implementing the 10 tips included in Tool #1. And consider implementing any or all of the following extra tips.

---[# FIVE TIPS TO AMELIORATE JOB DEMANDS AND IMPROVE JOB QUALITY   ]---

In addition to detracting from productivity, excessive job demands interfere with the enjoyment of our work, that is, Job Quality. These five tips were developed to address both issues. As with the previous tool's tips, think about how you can adapt these suggestions and examples to your workplace.

Tip 1: Make work more meaningful by applying your organization's core competencies in creative ways.

Try to identify a synergy between your products and services and your employees' values: home, family, recreation, education, giving back to the community, and so on. For example, Motorola uses its own senior technical staff to conduct in-house technical training courses, some of which are part of accredited M.S. degree programs. A construction company could provide home repairs for their employees.

What expertise does *your* organization have that could be made available to enhance your employees' personal or professional lives?

Some hotels allow their employees' children to watch television in an unrented room while their parent is working. Could you do anything like this at your workplace? For example, perhaps you could utilize available space and employees to provide ad hoc child care during school holidays. And if disaster strikes, offer your products and services—and volunteers from your workforce—to provide aid.

Tip 2: Effectively communicate the mission and vision of your organization.

One of the five principle reasons employees leave their jobs is: "It doesn't feel good around here." They do not get, or do not agree with, their employer's reason for being.

If you don't already have a mission statement that is short and to the point, distinguishes you from other organizations, and is inspiring, develop one!

For example, the mission statement of our training firm is:

Our Mission: To help you protect and optimize
your greatest asset—your people.

All the services provided by our firm are in execution of this mission.
Consider a vision statement as well. This should be very short. In a
sense, it's a loftier, "reach-out" version of the mission statement—the ideal
toward which your organization aspires.

For example, for our firm it is:

Our Vision: Organizational success in perfect accord
with individual fulfillment.

We constantly strive to develop solutions for our clients that contribute to their bottom line and enhance the quality of their employees'
lives.

Once you have a mission and/or vision statement, don't bury it in a
desk drawer. Communicate it and reiterate it to all stakeholders, especially to your employees. For example, our local fire station posts its mission
prominently above the station entrance. Our own mission or vision statement appears on our business cards, in each newsletter issue, as part of our
e-mail signature, and on our brochure. You may have noticed that our
vision appears in the dedication of this book. You'll see our mission again
in the Afterword.

Ensure that your mission is consistently adhered to by all. Employees
should constantly be asking themselves to what extent their actions are
contributing to the fulfillment of the mission. And managers should be
evaluating their staffs by the same criterion.

Tip 3: Link the mission and the job to the talents and aspirations of each employee.

In *The Truth About Burnout* (1997), Maslach and Leiter determine that one
of the main causes of burnout is job mismatch (or culture misfit). The
characteristics of the job are not a good match for the employee's talents.
Or the perceived purpose and values of the employer clash with those of
the employee. (Notice the word "perceived" in the context of Tip #2.)

Make hiring and promotion decisions based on:

- Relevant talent (that is, basic abilities, aptitudes, and inclinations), more than on skills or experience. The need for specific skills changes rapidly and talented employees can acquire skills and experience.
- Culture fit. And no, we are not talking about superficial attributes like race, gender, age, and so on. Rather, we refer to the more significant and relevant attribute of values.
- Temperament and lifestyle—as relevant to the position. For example, don't expect an introvert to be happy or successful as a telemarketer. A job requiring extensive travel or weekend work may not be suitable for an individual with parental obligations. (**Warning**: Don't make assumptions. Instead, ensure that the individual is crystal clear about the job requirements.)

Cascade the mission: Articulate it with increasing and relevant detail for each organizational unit. Flesh it out with goals and action plans for every individual manager and employee that also address that person's unique abilities and ambitions.

Do all of this for your entire workforce—part-timers, temps, and contractors as well. These days, more and more members of your workforce are other than regular, full-time employees. Far too often, these others feel left out and treated as second-class citizens.

Tip 4: Ensure that all employees have sufficient autonomy to deal with the challenges they face in their jobs.

As Cindy Ventrice, author of *Make Their Day!* (2003), observes:

> Difficult challenges—coupled with a lack of control—create frustration, job burnout, poor performance, and turnover.
>
> But those very same challenges—when coupled with the ability to make meaningful changes—create enthusiasm, peak performance, and loyalty.

Most employees want to do a good job. But when they are frustrated by too many rules, red tape, or micromanaging supervisors, their spirits plunge, performance suffers, and the best among them look for other opportunities.

Notice the threefold benefit resulting from this example of increased autonomy (reported by Bob Nelson in *1001 Ways to Energize Employees*):

Nurses at San Diego's Scripps Mercy Hospital have been given the authority to perform numerous patient-related tasks formerly reserved to specialized techs. This gain in autonomy has:

1. Energized the nurses

2. Improved patient care

3. Allowed management to cut seven layers of supervision down to four

Here is a cutting-edge example (also from Nelson's book):

The Mirage and Treasure Island Hotels operate under a system of "planned insubordination." All supervisors must explain to employees not only what to do but why they should do it. If the explanation is not satisfactory, the employee can refuse to do the task.

Sound risky? Well, the risk has had its reward. The hotels have a turnover rate of 12 percent—less than half the industry average.

Tip 5: Reciprocate *for the greater demands you place on employees.*

Notice the specific factors included in Job Demands in the 1997 National Study. All of these curtail employees' personal lives. Balance this by providing opportunities to deal with personal demands and desires.

Encourage employees to interact with family and friends during work hours. We realize that this is in direct opposition to typical practices, but those practices are based on an out-of-date, 9-to-5 paradigm.

So, permit personal phone calls. Allow family and friends to access the workplace, and not just during an annual Bring-Your-Son-or-Daughter-to-Work Day. Allow employees to access personal e-mail and nonwork websites, at least during rest breaks and lunch hour. Banning access to obscene or violent sites is fine, but don't get carried away.

Be generous in providing time off to handle personal needs (e.g., doctors' appointments, day-care arrangements, etc.).

Establish and encourage use of an Employee Assistance Program

(EAP). We find that most larger employers have an EAP, usually outsourced, but they utilize it insufficiently. The better EAPs can assist employees with a wide range of personal demands, far beyond alcoholism or drug abuse.

Encourage employees to establish clubs and special interest groups at work that meet on the employer's property after hours or during meal breaks. Limit your restrictions on such clubs to just basic human rights violations. For example, prohibit child pornography and hate groups, but permit men's, women's, and gay/bisexual/lesbian/transsexual (GBLT) groups.

APPLICATION

1. In what ways have the demands placed on your employees *increased* during the past 5-to-10 years?
   - Are they working longer hours? Bringing more work home?
   - Are they expected to accomplish more? Multitasking?
   - Are there fewer of them to do it (i.e., have you been downsizing)?
   - Are more of them working during shifts other than the traditional 9-to-5?

2. How have these increased demands *impacted* your workplace and employees?
   - Do they appear to be stressed out?
   - Are they spending less time with family and friends?
   - Does your team seem to be accomplishing less?
   - Are there increased interpersonal and/or interdepartmental frictions?

3. What can be *done* about it?
   - What ideas from this tool can be implemented at your workplace?
   - What new ideas or adaptations can you develop?
   - How much of this is in your direct control?
   - How can you influence the powers that be to make changes?

4. *Do* it!

TOOL THREE

3

Balance Their Work and Life

In the Introduction to Part 1, we presented the results of an ongoing 60-year study: "What Employees Want from Their Jobs." We highlighted the two factors that employees consistently rank at the very top:

1. Full appreciation for work done
2. Feeling in on things

Take a second look at that study. Notice what employees rank as number 3: Sympathetic help on personal problems. This phrasing is a bit archaic (the study began back in 1946); today, this probably would be called something like Sensitivity to work/life issues. And it's even more important to today's employees.

In Tools #1 and #2, we introduced the National Study of the Changing Workforce, conducted every five years by the Families and Work Institute. We drew your attention to three sets of factors examined in the 1997 study that have a significant impact on work outcomes—Job Quality, Job Demands, and Workplace Support.

In 2002, the National Study focused on Workplace Support, specifically of work/life issues. The study found:

Work–life supports on the job are powerfully related to positive
work outcomes—job satisfaction, commitment to employer, and
retention.

Three types of support were examined: flexible work arrangements,
work/life culture, and supervisor support. All three types are significant,
but the most powerful is *supervisor* support, especially on commitment.

**Figure 3-1. Supervisor Support of Personal/Family Needs
Related to Commitment to Employer in 2002.**

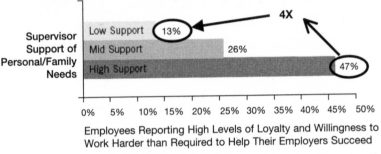

Employees Reporting High Levels of Loyalty and Willingness to
Work Harder than Required to Help Their Employers Succeed

SOURCE: *The Changing Workforce: Highlights of the (2002) National Study,* Families and Work Institute, No.
3, 2002.

Notice that four times as many employees with high supervisor support
had strong commitment to their employers. And commitment to employer translates to high levels of loyalty and a willingness to work harder than
required to help their employers succeed.

Would you like not only to retain your employees but also to have
them work harder? Well, take advantage of this tool's **Secret**:

Provide supervisory support for employees' work/life issues.

The 2002 National Study's report concludes with the observation:

Interestingly, none of these work/life supports necessarily imposes
direct costs upon employers, in contrast with conventional benefits.

Your organization does not need to be rolling in money to dramatically improve job satisfaction, loyalty, commitment, or retention.

If you are a senior executive or someone in HR with clout who can influence the flexible work arrangements or work/life culture of your organization, for goodness sake, do so. But you don't need to be in order to have a powerful impact on the loyalty and performance of your own team.

The National Study uses five measures of supervisor support, which we have converted into our...

FIVE PRINCIPLES FOR BALANCING WORK AND LIFE

Principle #1: Really care about the effects that work demands have on your employees' personal and family life.

Your employees can tell if you really do care. If, in all honesty, you don't care, you might want to reread the Introduction to this book. And also think about the practical results of such caring.

This principle sets the stage for the remaining four.

Principle #2: Never show favoritism when responding to employees' personal needs.

This does not mean always going by the book. For example, "Bereavement leave is three days (no more, no less) and is limited to the following familial relationships..."

It does mean evenhandedly assessing the significance (to the individual) of each employee's work/life issue, collaborating with that employee to develop a workable and perhaps creative solution, and weighing the impact of that solution on your enterprise and on other employees.

Principle #3: Bend over backward to accommodate employees when they have personal or family business to take care of.

This could range anywhere from approving an extended lunch hour for a doctor's appointment (for the employee or family member) to flexible work schedules to assistance with day care, and so on.

There are some accommodations you may not be able to make. Most important is to try, and to inform the employee that you have done so and why you cannot accommodate.

Principle #4: Demonstrate understanding when employees talk about personal or family issues that affect their work.

Put on your fellow-human-being hat when listening to employees' work/life concerns. How would you feel in that situation? How have you felt in similar situations?

Even if circumstances do not permit you to provide an ideal solution, just knowing that you really do understand will go a long way in engaging the employee's loyalty.

Principle #5: Ensure that employees feel comfortable bringing up family or personal issues with you as their supervisor.

If you adhere to the first four principles, this one will fall into place naturally. Also, Tool #7 on inquiry and active listening will help.

APPLICATION

1. *Meet* with each individual on your team, starting with:
   - The employee you'd most hate to lose...and/or
   - The employee you're most in danger of losing
2. *Ask* them about their work/life challenges.
   - Do they ever feel that their personal life is being shortchanged?
   - Do they ever feel like they're walking on a tightrope, balancing their work and personal lives?
   - What would they like to see more of from you? (Prepare to respond nondefensively.)
   - What accommodations might be helpful?
3. Brainstorm and *collaborate* with them to develop solutions. For example:

- Alternate work schedules or shift changes
- More flexibility in their hours
- More flexibility on your part
- Working from home to a reasonable extent
- Confidential consultation with your Employee Assistance Program

4. *Investigate* the feasibility of the solution(s) and *implement*...or
5. Tell the employee about your investigation and explain *why* you cannot accommodate.

2

Different Strokes

INDIVIDUAL DIFFERENCES

Part 1 presented basic principles and techniques applicable to virtually all employees, certainly to good employees.

We necessarily spoke in generalities, painting a picture using broad strokes. In a sense, we treated employees as if they were all the same. This, of course, is not the case. There are individual differences, as well as differences among groupings of individuals (e.g., generations, genders, ethnic groups, etc.)

Any remarks about groupings of people are themselves generalities, (e.g., Baby Boomers are preparing for retirement, men are from Mars, Latinos are more family-oriented than Anglos, etc.) Such generalities can have value, as long as plenty of room is made for individual differences within the group, thereby avoiding stereotypes.

Part 2 fine-tunes the observations made in Part 1 by exploring some of those differences: "different strokes for different folks" (a popular phrase from when Baby Boomers were young).

Two of the most significant differences among individuals are ability and personality.

Abilities differ in both type and degree. For example, some people have an athletic ability. Of those athletes, some have a particular affinity for golf. And golfers differ in degree of ability. Some are weekend golfers, some are professionals, and one is Tiger Woods.

In the workplace, there are many testing instruments that have been developed to assess the nature and degree of an employee's, especially a *potential* employee's, abilities. (Appendix C discusses the assessment of leadership abilities.) In most cases, however, the nature and degree of an employee's abilities are readily apparent from that person's work.

Personality is another type of difference among people. Various instruments have been developed to assess it. Two of the best known are Myers–Briggs Type Indicator (MBTI) and Dominance–Influence–Steadiness–Conscientiousness (DISC). We are more familiar with MBTI.

For example, an Introvert–Intuitive–Thinking–Perceiving (INTP)—who also is highly intelligent—probably would make a good scientist. An Extrovert–Sensing–Feeling–Judging (ESFJ) might be a good teacher or nurse.

An exploration of the assessment and workplace ramifications of ability and personality, although relevant to a leader, is outside the scope of this book. (If the reader is interested in either of these subjects, there are many books and websites available, some of which are listed in the Resource Guide for Part 2 at the end of the book.)

Instead, we focus on three issues of special relevance to today's workplace.

Tool #4 unlocks workplace diversity: what it really means, its various dimensions, the changing workforce, differing perceptions, preconceptions, stereotypes, and how to embrace diversity in your workplace.

Tool #5 opens up differences among generations, specifically the four generations currently in today's workplace: Traditionalists, Baby Boomers, Generation X, and Millennials. We examine the events and experiences that shape each generation's worldview and values, potential conflicts between generations, and the most effective ways to communicate with each.

Tool #6 is focused on people with disabilities and reveals how to comply with the Americans with Disabilities Act (ADA). We explain the rationale and essence of ADA, comment on appropriate language, introduce four core concepts, define and explain key terms and provisions, and outline your responsibilities as a leader.

Embrace Diversity

"We didn't all come over in the same ship, but we're all in the same boat."
—BERNARD M. BARUCH

Over the years, we all have observed increasing polarizations or schisms in our society. A classic one that has always been with us is rich versus poor (although in the modern era, we would phrase it as the fully employed versus the homeless and those on welfare). But even among the fully employed (i.e., in the workplace), yet more troubling schisms exist:

- Related to race and ethnic group...even subethnic groups
- Between generations...and genders
- Around hot-button issues, like abortion, stem cell research, creationism, and gay marriage...even smoking

This tool cannot eliminate such schisms, but it can *bridge* them, effectively and nonviolently.

DIVERSITY: MYTH AND REALITY

Many people regard diversity with some skepticism; as a fad or a code word for affirmative action. The reality is that diversity is one of the most fundamental and significant issues of the American workplace. The first thing to know about diversity is that it is not, or should not, be a code word for affirmative action.

Our ancestors did some pretty horrible things to each other: slavery, the subjugation of women, the virtual annihilation of Native Americans, and, more recently, forced segregation and exclusion. Affirmative action is based on the premise that the descendants of the victimizers are responsible for their ancestors' actions and should take steps to redress those wrongs by providing government-mandated preferential treatment to the descendants of the victims.

Affirmative action is not without controversy. It has its ardent supporters and its critics. But that's not what diversity is about. Each of us certainly is responsible for our own actions. And our primary responsibility is to recognize reality and deal with it appropriately.

Thus, our *Secret*:

> Understand the true nature of the American
> workforce...and the true meaning of diversity.

The clichéd image of the American population (and workforce) is a *melting pot* of homogeneous sameness in which people of different genders, races, and heritage are assimilated. A far more accurate image is a *salad bowl* of heterogeneous variety in which the ingredients (unique individuals) are integrated while the special flavor (identity) of each is maintained.

Which brings us to the true meaning of diversity:

- *All* the ways we are different from (and similar to) each other
- Our *perceptions* and *opinions* about those differences
- How we *treat* people based on those perceptions and opinions

Diversity is not a social problem to be solved, but a business opportunity to be optimized, for example, an expanded customer base, a broader source of employee talent, or a more harmonious workplace. And it's not just another fad; diversity is the way things are.

Diversity is a reality to be embraced.

DIFFERENT FROM AND SIMILAR TO EACH OTHER

"Consider the implications: If every single living thing is different from every other thing, then diversity becomes life's one irreducible fact.

Only variations are real...and to see them, you simply have to open your eyes.**"**
—ALFRED KINSEY

There are myriad ways individuals are different from and similar to each other. Some of them are shown in Figure 4-1.

Figure 4-1. Dimensions of Diversity.

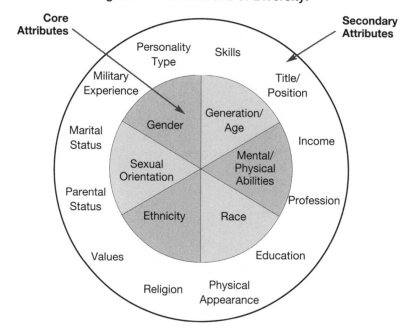

Adapted from: *Implementing Diversity* by Marilyn Loden, McGraw-Hill, 1996.

As you look at the attributes in the inner circle, think about what they have in common. We submit that these are fixed and therefore are not subject to individual choice. As we have labeled them, they are *core* attributes.(Age, of course, changes over time, but it is not subject to choice; and one's birthdate and generation never change. Some aspects of gender can be changed, but not at a fundamental chromosomal or procreational level. And any debate about sexual orientation versus preference is outside the scope of this book, and, we maintain, outside the scope of appropriate discourse in the workplace.)

What about the attributes in the outer ring? What do they have in common? These can and do change over time, and are subject to individual choice and/or societal influence. Also, many of these *secondary* attributes are related to and derived from the core attributes. For example, ethnicity and race are reflected in physical appearance and, often, religion, and someone's mental and physical abilities will influence his or her skills, position, income, profession, and education.

There is a certain irony in these two dimensions. With one significant exception, most prejudice, bias, and intolerance are based on core attributes. The one significant exception is religion. This is perhaps because much religious intolerance appears to be rooted in ethnic differences. Also, although one's religion is subject to choice, for most people, it is virtually a core attribute.

However, most of us would say that who we really are as unique individuals lies in our secondary attributes. For example, two shy, single, computer programmers have more in common, even if one is a 35-year-old Asian man and the other is a 25-year-old white woman, than an extroverted secretary of state and an introverted seamstress, both of whom are African American women in their fifties.

APPLICATION #1

1. Complete the **My Diversity Dimensions** activity (see Worksheet 4-1) about yourself.
    *   Be as vague as you like (e.g., for Income, Age, or Religion).
    *   Reveal only what you choose to. (Notice we have not included sexual orientation.)

Worksheet 4-1. My Diversity Dimensions.

Attribute	I am...
Core	
Gender	
Age/Generation	
Inherent Abilities	
Race	
Ethnicity	
Secondary	
Personality Type	
Skills	
Title/Position	
Income	
Profession	
Education	
Appearance	
Religion	
Values	
Parental Status	
Marital Status	
Military Experience	

- When in doubt, write your self-perception (e.g., Inherent Abilities, Appearance, etc.).
2. Have others (e.g., coworkers, friends, spouse) complete the activity about themselves.
3. Review together your differences and similarities.
4. Did you learn anything new about the other person? About yourself?

─┤ PERCEPTIONS AND PRECONCEPTIONS ├─

Look at this illustration. What do you see? Do you see a pretty young woman or an ugly old hag? Perhaps both?

Show this illustration to others. Do they all see the same thing? Who's right? Who's wrong?

The answer, of course, is that no one is wrong. Both images have been built into the illustration. The point here is that some of our perceptions may be different, but equally valid.

However, some of our perceptions may not be valid.

What is this a picture of?

That's easy. It's a map of the world.

Or is it?

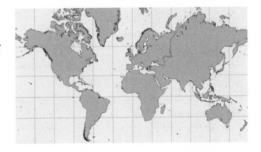

What about this picture?

Whoa! It's upside down.

Or is it?

After all, why should north be at the top of the world?

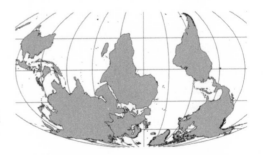

In order to make some comparisons, let's look at this in the conventional north-on-top orientation.

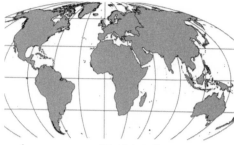

Still looks kind of distorted, doesn't it?

In fact, however, this Mollweide equal area projection (created by mathematician and astronomer Karl Mollweide in the early nineteenth century) shows landmasses in their *true* proportions to each other.

That first world map (the familiar-looking one) is a Mercator projection, created way back in the sixteenth century by the German cartographer Gerardus Mercator. Understandably, from his point of view, he placed Europe in the center of the map.

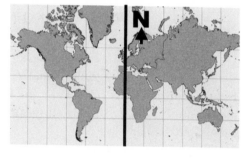

However, for over 400 years, Mercator's Eurocentric view has dominated the way the world has been represented on maps, including those used in twentieth-century American classrooms—thereby forming our preconception of the world.

But Eurocentrism and north-on-top (also reflected in the Mollweide and most other projections) are not the only biases built into this map.

Let's look at these two projections side by side. Our preconception is on the left and reality is on the right. Since no one lives in Antarctica but a few scientists, we have omitted this continent (and some of the Pacific Ocean) for our current purposes.

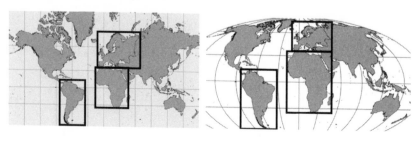

Notice on the Mercator projection on the left how Europe seems to be slightly larger than South America. The reality (on the right) is that South America (6.9 million square miles) is twice as large as Europe (3.8 million square miles).

Our preconception of Europe and Africa is that they are about the same size. Right? Wrong! In fact, Africa (11.6 million square miles) is *three times* the size of Europe (3.8 million square miles)!

Many of our preconceptions about the world, in this case, its geography, are at odds with reality. And it's not just our view of world geography that is skewed, but also our view of the American workforce.

—————| **OUR CHANGING WORLD** |—————

Or, as we put it: This is not your father's workforce.

A hundred years ago, less than one-fifth of the U.S. workforce was female. By the 1950s (in a Baby Boomer's father's day), it had risen to about one-third, but virtually all in support functions, or what used to be called "pink collar."

Today, women represent approximately half of American workers, and not just in lower-paid support jobs, but in the professional and managerial ranks as well, and in all kinds of nontraditional roles.

Those of us who are Baby Boomers have witnessed, or experienced, dramatic changes in women's roles. Even younger generations have seen and will continue to see changes in race/ethnic demographics.

Did you graduate from high school by 1990? If so, you were either already in or preparing for the workforce.

At that time, only 25 percent of the U.S. population was nonwhite or minority, by which we mean African American, Asian, Latino, and/or Native American (Figure 4-2).

By 2025, 39 percent of Americans are projected to

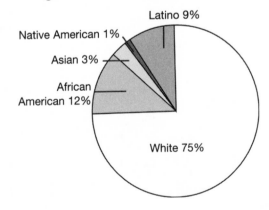

Figure 4-2. U.S. Population, 1990.

Latino 9%
Native American 1%
Asian 3%
African American 12%
White 75%

be minorities (which is steadily becoming a misleading designation). There will be virtually no change in the percentage of Native Americans and the percentage of Africans Americans will increase somewhat.

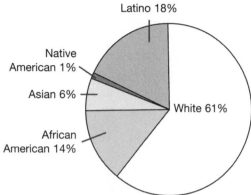

Figure 4-3. U.S. Population, 2025.

But the percentages of Americans who are Asian or Latino are expected to double! By the way, as of 2003, Latinos became the second largest race/ethnic group in the country.

And not all Americans are native-born.

There was a major influx of immigrants early in the twentieth century so that by 1930, 12 percent of the U.S. population was foreign-born. But by 1970, when Boomers began entering the workforce, this number dropped to 5 percent. Since then, however, it has doubled to 10 percent.

The real change in immigration, however, has been where people have emigrated from.

During the first half of the twentieth century, the vast majority (83 percent) of foreign-born Americans came from Europe. Visualize the Ellis Island scene from *Godfather II* or the steerage passengers in the movie *Titanic*. As of 1990, however, less than one-fourth were from Europe. Most of the others have been from Asia (26 percent) and, especially, Latin America (44 percent).

In your father's day, the image of the workforce was all-American white male. Today, native-born white males represent less than half of American workers, and only about 25 percent of those entering the workforce. The other 75 percent are women, people of color, and immigrants.

All of these changes can be very disorienting. Some of our preconceptions just don't fit anymore.

But how many of us are still doing business based on an out-of-date paradigm? To what extent is our own behavior—and corporate America's HR policies, recruiting practices, marketing strategies, and management styles—based on the assumption of a one-size-fits-all homogeneous workforce and customer base?

—⌐   **A RIDDLE**   ⌐—

Bobby and his father are in a horrible car accident, which instantly kills Bobby's father. Bobby is seriously injured and rushed to the hospital. The surgeon takes one look at Bobby on the operating table and says: "Oh my God! I can't operate on this boy...he's my son!"

How can this be?

Please do not read further until you've taken time to ponder this.

We have posed this riddle in our training workshops and newsletter. Before revealing the solution, here are some of the interesting answers we've received:

- The deceased father was the birth father and the surgeon is his stepfather or adoptive father (or vice versa). ← most common answer

- The deceased "father" is Bobby's priest. ← most creative

- The boy was misidentified by the hospital. ← most cynical

- There are two boys named Bobby. ← simplest (other than the intended solution)

- The surgeon is the adoptive father of Bobby's twin, separated at birth. ← most convoluted

- The father who was killed was the sperm donor. ← our favorite

It's amazing to what lengths the human mind will go when faced with a paradox.

The solution to the riddle is: The surgeon is Bobby's *mother*! Did you get it? Don't be embarrassed if you didn't. Most people don't. We've even stumped a few women doctors with it.

What do you think is the point of the riddle?

Of course you "know" that women can be surgeons. But your subconscious does not. Remember the portrayals of surgeons on television as you were growing up and any surgeon you may have known as a child. Were *any* of them women? (If you are Gen Y, perhaps some of them were women, in which case you may not appreciate why this is a riddle to older folks.) It was these early life experiences that formed your gut-level image of a surgeon.

Many of our preconceptions are very deeply seated and may be influencing our thoughts and behaviors, regardless of how enlightened we are.

The more consciously aware of these preconceptions we become, the more our thoughts and behaviors will be under our control, rather than being controlled by outside factors as when we were children.

HOW WE TALK TO OURSELVES

Some of our perceptions—those preconceptions like the Mercator map, our father's workforce, and the surgeon—are incorrect, or at least out of date. Some, like the perceptions elicited by the ambiguous illustration, are just different, but equally valid.

We would like you now to take a private look at some of your own perceptions. And it is a private look; do not show what you write to anyone else.

As you look at each word listed in Worksheet 4-2, a conversation or image will form in your mind. In the Impression column, briefly describe the picture, words, or scene that comes spontaneously to mind.

Under Opinion, note how you feel about each item, for example, like/dislike, good/bad, beautiful/ugly, and so on.

Under Origin, note where you first got your idea or feeling, or where you think it may have come from.

Notice the two different responses in the example for the word "immigrant." The first is more positive, but it is no more valid than the second response.

If you choose not to complete the entire table, focus on those words that trigger the most vivid impressions and for which you have some type of opinion or feeling.

Do not censor or evaluate your own first impressions!

For this activity to have any value for you, not censoring yourself is very important. This is not a test of political correctness. You are neither good nor bad because of what your gut reaction and your culture say. It is what you do with these thoughts later that counts.

Worksheet 4-2.

WORD	IMPRESSION	OPINION	ORGIN
EXAMPLE: immigrant	*person on a boat* **OR** *unshaven worker*	*good, brave* **OR** *bad, scary*	*grandma's story* **OR** *dad avoided them*
girls			
boys			
career women			
gays			
lesbians			
arabs			
indians			
jews			
handicapped			
old people			
latinos			
oriental			
white men			
black			

Adapted from: *Working Together* by Dr. George Simons, Crisp, 1994.

After you finish this activity, we suggest that you put on your enlightened, politically correct hat and review what you wrote.

What was this experience like for you? How do you feel about your uncensored reactions—any sense of discomfort, embarrassment, or shame? If so, remember that you are responsible only for your actions, not for your deeply seated preconceptions. Do not judge yourself harshly.

Instead, think about those preconceptions. Try to become more aware of them as you interact with others. Whenever you realize that you are experiencing a reaction you don't consciously agree with, challenge it in your mind. Remind yourself of the reality; for example, "No, some surgeons are women."

We'll say more about this when we talk about breaking down stereotypes.

STEREOTYPES: YESTERDAY AND TODAY

Many of our stereotypes were formed by the media, especially movies and television. Let's examine some stereotypes from the past and see how they have changed over time.

Beginning with female stereotypes, think of the characters Scarlett O'Hara and Mammy from *Gone With the Wind*. Mammy certainly was a classic stereotype of the nonwhite woman. In the story (1860s), she was a slave, but her servant role accurately reflected the times of the movie's premiere (1939) and for decades thereafter.

Today, that role is portrayed not as much by African American women, but by Latino women, such as in the movies *Maid in Manhattan* and *Spanglish*.

Scarlett O'Hara, although she had lots of spirit, portrayed white women as flighty and interested mainly in looking pretty and getting a man. Today, we have the four women from *Sex and the City*. Although they have professions, their primary interests seem to be looking pretty and getting a man.

Katharine, in the TV show *CSI*, is an interesting modern stereotype. As a forensic crime scene investigator, she is a professional in a nontraditional role. (She is also an example of a recent trend of portraying middle-aged women as still being "sexy.") But the character's former occupation was stripper. This is not an occupation that most professional women identify with.

Moving on to male stereotypes...

The classic white male stereotype is probably John Wayne—brave, strong, independent, and emotionally closed off.

An African American male stereotype from somewhat earlier was Stepin Fetchitshuffling, subservient, ignorant, and eager to please.

What are modern portrayals of white and African American men? Now they are often paired in buddy movies like *48 Hours* and *Men in Black*. The African American portrayals have evolved quite a bit. Now they are intelligent, rebellious, wise-cracking, and almost equal partners to the whites. ("Almost," because they typically are portrayed as the younger, junior partners.)

What can we say about the white men in these movies? Brave, strong, independent, and emotionally closed off.

Our final example is Asian men...

A classic Asian male stereotype is Charlie Chan—wise, highly intelligent, but speaking in extremely broken English. And the actor portraying the character was always non-Asian.

Today, instead of Charlie Chan, we have Jackie Chan and Jet Li, Asian actors, and their speech has improved, but the stereotype has been dumbed down. Their competence now is with their fists.

HOW WE BUILD STEREOTYPES

How do we as individuals or as a culture form such stereotypes?

The human mind naturally groups similar experiences (especially early life experiences), categorizes, and labels them. We form opinions and judgments of these categories based on our experience. Sometimes these judgments are negative, but not always. For example, Charlie Chan was portrayed as very wise and insightful; many of the attributes associated with the John Wayne archetype (e.g., bravery and self-reliance) are admirable; and women often have been portrayed as nurturing, which is positive, although limiting.

Then we spend the rest of our lives looking for proof, subconsciously at least. When we see someone who somewhat fits the stereotype—for example, a woman who is interested in looking pretty and getting a man—we say to ourselves, in effect: "See, I told you so."

And the exceptions (e.g., Hillary Clinton) prove the rule: You are not like the rest of *them*.

It can become a ... self-fulfilling prophecy. Figure 4-4 diagrams the process.

Imagine that's you in the center of the oval—with your opinions and stereotypes, and maybe even biases and prejudices. These impact how you

Figure 4-4. Self-Fulfilling Prophecy.

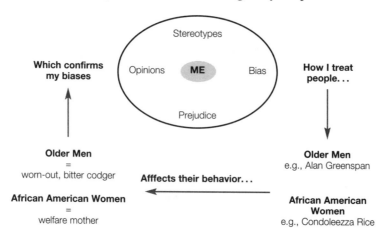

treat people, for example, older men and African American women. And that affects their behavior. So instead of an Alan Greenspan (who, as Federal Reserve Chairman until his recent retirement, was one of the most powerful men in the country), such treatment increases the chances of your encountering a worn-out, bitter old codger.

And instead of a Condoleezza Rice, one of the most powerful African American women in the country, you are more likely to find a welfare mother.

Which, of course, confirms the biases you started with. It is a vicious circle.

⎯⎯⎯[HOW TO BREAK DOWN STEREOTYPES]⎯⎯⎯

How do we break out of this circle or break down our stereotypes? You need to ask yourself:

- Does your opinion hold true for *everyone* in the group? Yes, some women are beauty queens, and some are surgeons.

- Is the person thought of as part of a *group* first, rather than as an individual? When you see Hillary Clinton on television, do you see Baby Boomer White Woman or a unique individual in American politics?

- Do your *past experiences* with members of this group affect this interaction? Most of those experiences stem from childhood, but some can be recent. For example, think about the impact of all of the images of Hurricane Katrina victims in 2005. Again and again, African Americans were associated with poverty, squalor, and helplessness. Unless you are African American, it may be necessary to consciously remind yourself of all the black men and women you know or have seen who are pretty much like you.

- And here's a question that is especially relevant for the workplace: Does your opinion reflect the knowledge, skills, and abilities necessary to *do the job*? For example, do you view people in wheelchairs as cripples or as unique individuals with one obvious mobility limitation and all kinds of abilities? (See the next tool.)

APPLICATION #2

Think about your organization and workplace. As an individual or as a leadership team, reflect on the following questions:

1. Are we *excluding* potential customers or employees?
   - Which groups (e.g., women, race/ethnic groups, older people, people with disabilities, etc.)?
   - Is it because of our communications?

2. Is our *workforce* representative of all our customers?
   - At all levels?
   - In all functions?
   - Is this a problem?

3. Are there *intergroup* tensions, frictions, or misunderstandings?
   - Which groups (e.g., men–women, whites–nonwhites, Boomers–Gen X/Y, etc.)?
   - In certain functions more than others?
   - What types of problems?

4. Does *every* individual feel included, accepted, and understood?

5. What is all of this *costing* our organization/my department?

6. What can I (or we) *do* about it? What do I (or we) *want* to do about it?

5

Get a Grip on Generations

Tool #4 opened up the issue of workplace diversity and explored many of its manifestations, but concentrated especially on gender, race, and ethnic differences.

Another significant way in which we are different from or similar to each other is our *generation*...or, as we put it...

Who you are now is *what* you were *when*.

Note: This is our own phrase, but it was inspired by a wonderful training video we saw many years ago, *What You Are Is Where You Were When*, by Morris Massey. See the Resource Guide for information about his recently updated version.

The events and conditions we experience during our formative years help define who we are and how we view the world.

As stated in the introduction to Part 2, any remarks about groupings of people are themselves generalities. With this tool we make some sweeping generalizations based on the years when people were children or adolescents. Even the range of birth years assigned to generations varies, depending on who is doing the categorizing.

However, every individual is unique and a person's generation is only one factor that has influenced that person. And one's position within a generation modifies the extent to which observations are applicable. You probably will see yourself and others fitting these generalizations to *some* extent.

FOUR GENERATIONS AT WORK

Right now, there are four generations in the American workplace:

1. Traditionalists (also known as the Greatest Generation or the Silent Generation) are usually defined as those born between 1925 and 1945 and who are now in their sixties or older. (Most of this generation is no longer in the workplace. Those who still are were born toward the end of that period and may have more in common with the next generation than with their older fellow Traditionalists.)

2. Baby Boomers (or simply, Boomers) are those born between 1946 and 1963 and who are now in their fifties (or late forties or early sixties).

3. Generation X (or simply, Gen X) includes those born between 1964 and 1978 and who are now in their thirties or early forties.

4. Millennials (or Gen Y) are those born after 1978 and who are now in their twenties or late teens (or have not yet entered the workplace).

Notice that the span of years for generations has become increasingly shorter. This is due to an increasing rate of change, spurred especially by technology. This (and longer life/working spans) has created the unprecedented phenomenon of four distinct generations at work together.

SHARED EXPERIENCES

Each generation grew up exposed to a different set of events and conditions that influenced its members' values and perspectives. Let's examine some of the categories of experiences each generation had and look for commonalities and contrasts.

Media and Technology

Traditionalists (Radio Babies) watched newsreels at the movies, listened to the radio in the living room, and occasionally spoke with friends on rotary telephones. The defining workplace technology of their youth was the assembly line. Later in life, they learned that "surfing" was something like water skiing.

Baby Boomers (TV Babies) watched a choice of three evening news programs on television, listened to transistor radios in various locations, and frequently chatted with friends on touch-tone telephones. The defining workplace technology of their youth was mainframe computers. "Surfing" to a Boomer meant The Beach Boys and *The Endless Summer*.

Generation X (Computer Babies) watched a wide range of news coverage (including 24-hour cable), listened to their Walkman on the street, and chatted with friends at length on their cell phones. The defining workplace (and home) technology of their youth was the personal computer. "Surfing" to Gen X meant rapidly changing television channels with a remote control.

Millennials (iPod Babies) have been watching myriad choices of news coverage on mobile devices, listening to their iPods everywhere, and continuously texting friends on their advanced cell phones. The defining workplace/home/cafe technology has been the Internet, which, of course, they have been "surfing."

The media and technology of Gen X and Millennials have more in common than that of previous generations.

Significant Events

Traditionalists grew up during the Great Depression, World War II, and the Korean War—long-term traumatic events that brought Americans together and were successfully resolved (although to a lesser extent in Korea) after extended hardship. However, most Traditionalists currently in the workplace experienced only the Korean War.

Boomers faced the Cold War and the Vietnam War—also traumatic and extended, but which polarized the country, alienated Boomers from their parents, and were not successfully resolved (at least during their youth). They were repeatedly jolted by the assassinations of the 1960s and then later by Watergate.

Gen X witnessed the fall of the Berlin Wall and Desert Storm—events of shorter duration and less trauma than either of the previous two generations (or the following). Some also were affected by Watergate.

Millennials have had Columbine and 9/11—traumatic events of very short duration (but long-term impact), similar in nature to the assassinations of the 1960s. And they've also had the Iraq War, more similar to Vietnam (in some ways) and Desert Storm (in other ways) than to World War II.

The significant events of Boomers and Millennials seem to have more in common than those of the other generations. Those of Traditionalists and Gen X seem to be somewhat unique.

Social Change

For Traditionalists, it was the New Deal; for Boomers, the sexual revolution ("sex, drugs, and rock n' roll"), and the civil rights movement. For Gen X, it was women's liberation. And for Millennials, it has been technology and the speed of change.

The nature of the social changes experienced by Boomers and Gen X was similar, having to do with gender and race roles. Gen X and Millennials shared the impact of women's lib (and a higher divorce rate) on homelife. Many were "latchkey kids."

Transportation and Energy

All four generations grew up with the automobile. Traditionalists witnessed the growth of air travel, hydroelectric power, and increased use of petroleum as gasoline. Boomers experienced the apparent birth of the space age and nuclear age and saw new applications of petroleum (e.g., the "plastics!" line from *The Graduate*). Gen X witnessed problems with the space program and nuclear energy and with both the sources and environmental consequences of petroleum. Millennials have seen a dramatic cutback to the space program and nuclear power, a continuing energy crisis, and a seriously threatened environment.

Traditionalists and Boomers shared similar themes of growth and optimism. Gen X and Millennials have shared themes of decline and pessimism.

Pop Culture

Traditionalists swooned to Frank Sinatra and danced to the big bands. Boomers fainted at Elvis and danced to Motown, and then smoked grass to the Beatles. Gen X moonwalked with Michael Jackson and danced to disco. We confess to being out of touch with the music and dance of Millennials and merely observe phenomena like Britney Spears and rap.

VALUES AND EXPECTATIONS

Experiences during childhood and adolescence influence the values and expectations of each generation. It is here that our generalizations become quite sweeping. Take them with many grains of salt.

Traditionalists' approach to the job tends to be hard work and sacrifice. Boomers also work hard, but for success. Gen X tends toward entrepreneurship. Millennials' motto is "Show me the money." They've been described as "Gen X on steroids"—a pattern you will continue to see here.

Traditionalists tend to be motivated by duty and honor and climbing the career ladder. Boomers are more interested in a meaningful experience and personal growth. Gen X wants leisure time (they've been at the forefront of "work/life balance") and tends to be skeptical and pragmatic. Millennials crave stimulation and share Gen X's desire for leisure time, but more so.

Traditionalists like rules and order and are comfortable with formality and authority. Boomers rebelled against rules (especially those they regard as arbitrary) and prefer change and competition. Gen X likes independence and autonomy and is comfortable with informality (e.g., "business casual"). Millennials like rapid change and are very informal (e.g., t-shirts and flip-flops).

Traditionalists value privacy. In contrast, Boomers value teamwork. Gen X values techno literacy. Millennials value techno living.

Traditionalists are attracted to things (the expressions "status symbol" and "keeping up with the Joneses" originated with this generation). Boomers are attracted to causes. Gen X acquires information. Millennials are turned on by speed and flexibility.

Traditionalists have had few choices available eventually. Boomers have had more choices available sooner. Gen X expects many choices very soon. And Milliennials demand myriad choices now.

Each generation has an impact on the others. For example, our own allegiance to "respect" may be rooted more in Traditionalist values than in our own generation's (Boomers). And that impact is not only on those following but on their predecessors as well. For example, *everyone* today uses cellphones and expects more choices and greater work/life balance in the shorter term than they did years ago.

CONFLICT BETWEEN GENERATIONS

Generation gap is not new. The term was coined by Boomers in the 1960s to describe their alienation from their parents and "the establishment." What's new is that there now are gaps among the four generations that are simultaneously in the workplace.

This can create conflict or, at least, tension and confusion. For convenience, we provide a few simplified examples of potential conflict between two *groups* of generations: the younger Generation X and Millennials (Gen X and Gen Y) versus the older Traditionalists and Baby Boomers (Trads and Boomers):

Gen X and GenY	Trads and Boomers
"You're blocking my way!"	"Wait your turn!"
"Too much politicking…not enough work!"	"Can you spell naïve?"
"You're stuck in the hierarchy!"	"You have no respect for authority!"
"You're not current on technology!"	"You need to improve your influence skills!"
"Dress for comfort!"	"Dress for success!"
"#s look gd…lnch@1/ back l8r*"	"What?!"

* "The numbers look good. I'm going to lunch at 1 P.M. and I'll be back later. Right?"

Some of these are based more on age than generation. For example, older people (regardless of their generation) are viewed as the establishment and tend to be more conservative.

As we stated at the beginning of Tool #4, such gaps cannot be eliminated, but they can be bridged through understanding, flexibility, and, of course, respect.

─┤ HOW TO COMMUNICATE WITH... ├─

To communicate and interact effectively with anyone, it helps to know where the person is coming from and adjust your style as much as possible to what is most familiar and comfortable for that person.

Here are some tips for communicating with those *other* generations:

Traditionalists

- Be patient—the "silent generation" are private people, slow to open up.
- Focus on their words, not only body language.
- Communicate face-to-face…or in writing (hard copy).
- Do not waste their time.

Baby Boomers

- Be conscious of body language (yours and theirs).
- Speak in an open, direct style.
- Avoid controlling language.
- Answer questions thoroughly, with details.
- Present options to demonstrate flexibility.

Generation X

- Use e-mail primarily.
- Talk in short sound bites.
- Request and provide regular feedback.
- Share information regularly, keep them in the loop.
- Use an informal style.

Millennials

- Use e-mail or text messaging.
- Use action words…and challenge them.
- Request and provide frequent feedback.
- Do not talk down to them.
- Use humor, fun, and stimulation.
- Encourage risk taking and rule breaking.

6

Focus On Ability

The Americans with Disabilities Act (ADA) of 1990 has had the most far-reaching impact on the workplace since the Civil Rights Act of 1964. Yet many Americans remain uncertain about their rights and responsibilities under the law, such key terms as *disability*, *qualified*, and *reasonable accommodation*, and how to interact effectively and legally with persons with disabilities, in all aspects of employment.

This tool helps to eliminate such uncertainty and will enable you to comply fully with the law and forge a productive and harmonious workforce, affording equal opportunity to all.

WHY ADA?

Some 54 million Americans have a disability. Many of us will at some point during our life.

But as of 1990, when the ADA was passed, only one of three had a job and only one of four of those with a job worked full time. In case there is any doubt, the vast majority (83 percent according to one survey) want to work.

There are many heartwarming, inspirational stories of people with disabilities who have fulfilled their dreams due to ADA. Our personal favorite is about the professional golfer Casey Martin:

Casey Martin is a former NCAA golf champion with a circulatory
disorder that made his right leg extremely weak. This disability did
not interfere with his ability to swing the golf club, but it did require
him to use a golf cart to get around the course.

That was okay with the NCAA, but not with the PGA Tour...until
an ADA-based court ruling that was upheld by the Supreme Court
in 2001.

By the way, Casey's teammate in that 1994 NCAA Championship win
was none other than Tiger Woods. Who knows what Casey could have
achieved during those years that he was excluded from the circuit.

There has been considerable controversy surrounding this case, which
we will comment on shortly. Also, keep Casey's story in mind when we discuss essential job functions.

ESSENCE OF THE ACT

The ADA prohibits discrimination on the basis of disability in:

- State and local government
- Commercial facilities and public accommodations
- Transportation and telecommunications
- Educational institutions
- Employment

This tool relates to Title I of the Act, which deals with your responsibilities as an employer.

Note: If you work in the federal government, the Rehabilitation Act of
1973 is the applicable law. However, it was amended in 1992 to incorpo-
rate the same provisions as the ADA Title I described in this tool.

Title I requires employers with 15 or more employees to provide qualified individuals with disabilities an equal opportunity to benefit from the
full range of employment-related opportunities available to others.

Note: Employers do not have to hire someone with a disability over a
more qualified person without a disability. The goal of the ADA is to provide equal access and opportunities to individuals with disabilities, not to
give them an unfair advantage.

For example, Title I:

- Prohibits discrimination in recruitment, hiring, promotions, training, pay, social activities, and other privileges of employment

- Restricts questions that can be asked about an applicant's disability before a job offer is made

- Requires that employers make *reasonable accommodation* to the known physical or mental limitations of otherwise *qualified* individuals with *disabilities* (unless it results in undue hardship)

Each of the above *italicized* terms needs definition and clarification. But first, let's cover some core concepts and appropriate language.

APPROPRIATE LANGUAGE

Most of us are savvy enough to avoid such obviously demeaning terms as *crippled, blind as a bat*, and so on. But what is this person-with-a-disability business? What's wrong with the term *disabled person?* (Or *blind man, deaf woman, a paraplegic*, etc.)What's wrong with it is that it focuses on the disability rather than on the person and his or her abilities. The disability may indeed be relevant, for example, when providing reasonable accommodation, but it is secondary in importance to the person, as a human being and as a qualified employee with job skills.

It may be a new habit for many of us, but it is well worth the minor effort. So it's:

- Engineer with a hearing impairment, not deaf engineer
- Accountant in a wheelchair, not wheelchair-bound accountant
- Manager who is blind, not blind manager, and so on

Or, simply, Don, Sheryl, Ms. Grimme, and so on. By the way, *handicapped* also may not be an appropriate term. Many people believe it derives from nineteenth-century England, when persons with disabilities were forced to beg on the streets with cap in hand.

This discussion about language brings to light the first of our core concepts.

—[**FOUR CORE CONCEPTS**   ]—

Concept #1: Focus on ability!

The image we hold in our mind to underscore this concept is Stephen Hawking, who has an extremely disabling affliction...and is perhaps the most able person on the planet!

Notice a disability only as it may impact performing essential job functions or as requested by the person. (We revisit the term *essential* under Key Terms later in this tool.)

Concept #2: Challenge assumptions, prejudgment, and fear!

Virtually all of us have these, at least regarding disabilities with which we've had little or no experience. Stephen Hawking, for example, is unusual in appearance and his unaided speech is virtually impossible to understand. This may bring up feelings of fear and discomfort.

But our primary model for this concept is someone else: Christopher Reeve. After his accident in 1995 left him paralyzed from the neck down, most people assumed his career was over. He certainly challenged those assumptions—going on to deliver his most distinguished performances as an actor and director. His greatest achievement, however, was as a spokesperson for people with disabilities and an advocate for medical research.

Bringing this concept into the workplace, here is a true story we heard recently:

> A person in a wheelchair (and with no use of his hands) applied for a clerk-typist position. The HR manager put his assumptions on hold and told him simply that a typing test was required. The applicant leaned back in his wheelchair and proceeded to type 100 words per minute...with his toes!

Which takes us to our third concept...

Concept #3: Focus on what is to be done...not how or when!

As you will see, this gets to the essence of reasonable accommodation and impacts job descriptions, preemployment inquiries, scheduling, and day-to-day interactions. As you do this, you may need to...

Concept #4: Challenge tradition!

This relates back to the Casey Martin case. Most of the controversy surrounding this case stems from a challenge to a tradition of professional golf—"real" golfers walk the course. The lesson to be learned is that the courts expect employers to change their traditions of *how* the work is performed, when necessary to comply with the ADA.

In working with employers and with their employees, we find that the greatest single barrier to ADA compliance is this issue of clinging to traditions—even clinging to those that are not necessary to the performance of essential job functions or to accomplishing the organization's mission.

Think about the traditions of your organization and the professions in it. Which of them are getting in the way of ADA compliance and, reflecting back to Tool #4, in the way of fully embracing diversity?

Once you grasp these four core concepts, the myriad details of ADA and how to comply with it will fall into place.

KEY TERMS

With these concepts as a foundation, let's take a closer look at what the ADA means by *disability*, *qualified*, and *reasonable accommodation*.

Disability

> A disability is a physical or mental impairment that substantially limits one or more of the major life activities of such individual...or a record of such an impairment ...or being regarded as having such an impairment.

The ADA covers more than just people who are deaf, blind, or use wheelchairs. It also covers:

* People who have *physical* conditions, such as medical disorders, cosmetic disfigurement, and severe damage or loss to a body part or system.

  Examples include epilepsy, paralysis, diabetes, multiple sclerosis, HIV infection, or severe forms of arthritis, hypertension, or carpal tunnel syndrome—also alcoholism.

- People with *mental* impairments, such as mental illness or retardation, learning disabilities, and psychological disorders.

  Examples include major depression, bipolar (manic-depressive) disorder, dyslexia, and mental retardation.

But when dealing with ADA issues, you should avoid engaging in medical diagnosis. Instead, focus on the effect a disability has on a person's life. Which brings us to *major life activities*. Nothing mysterious here—seeing, hearing, speaking, walking, breathing, performing manual tasks, learning, caring for oneself, working, and so on.

Thus far, we have been talking about *actual* impairments. The ADA also covers:

- A person with a *record of* any such impairment.

  For example, cancer that is now in remission, a recovering alcoholic, or a person who has recovered from mental illness.

- A person who is *regarded as* having such impairment, particularly if you were to act based on myths, fears, or stereotypes.

  For example: Although AIDS is a disability, homosexuality is not. However, if an employer were to treat gay persons as if they had AIDS, that would be covered.

- A person who is *associated with* people with disabilities.

  For example: an employer who is concerned about excessive absenteeism or health insurance costs from a person whose spouse has a disability. Or someone who performs volunteer work for people with AIDS and there's an unwarranted fear of infection.

Not all physical or mental conditions are covered, however. The following are not protected under ADA:

- Minor, nonchronic conditions of short duration, such as a sprain, broken limb, or flu.

- Individuals who currently engage in the illegal use of drugs.

- Advanced age or pregnancy. (These are covered by other laws, but not as disabilities.)

- Compulsive gambling, kleptomania, and pyromania.

- Homosexuality, bisexuality, transvestitism, sexual behavior disorders. (Homosexuality and bisexuality are protected by many state and local laws, although not as disabilities.)

  Note: This grouping of sexual orientation with behavior *disorders* is as it is presented in federal government publications, not as we would have arranged it.

- Job performance limitations due strictly to environmental, cultural, or economic factors, such as poverty. (For example: Inability to read due to dyslexia is covered, but if due to lack of education, it is not covered.)

- Job performance problems due strictly to personality or character traits.

  (For example: irresponsibility, bad temper, computer phobia, and shyness.)

Qualified

This term pertains to an individual's ability to perform the essential functions of a job, with or without reasonable accommodation.

We discuss reasonable accommodation in some depth shortly. Let's first examine the term *essential*. Essential job functions are the reason a job exists and are required by the employer. This must be a justifiable requirement, not arbitrary. Typically, these functions are performed frequently. If not frequently, then significant consequences would result if the function is not performed or it is a specialized skill needed for the job, such as a police officer's use of a weapon.

Marginal (nonessential) job functions are not performed frequently or can be performed by other qualified personnel already on staff (without appreciably impacting their ability to perform their own essential job functions). Or, there will be no significant consequences if the job functions are not performed.

Reflecting back on Casey Martin, *walking* is performed frequently by professional golfers, but:

- Is it the reason for golf?
- Is it a specialized skill?
- What significant consequences would result if not performed?

Those who follow this sport tell us that there is a consequence. It relates to the fatigue incurred by walking the course. Whether it is a significant consequence is open to debate. And, of course, Casey experiences disproportionate fatigue just by standing and by walking from the cart path to the ball.

Whatever one's personal take on this controversy, the Supreme Court has determined that significant consequences would not result if Casey uses a golf cart instead of walking.

APPLICATION

1. Visualize a *typical job* that you supervise.

2. Identify the *essential* functions of that job. (**Hint:** They probably include those tasks for which employees in that job received training or special education.)

3. Identify the *marginal* functions of that job. (**Hint:** Think about some of the routine tasks or errands that really anyone could do.)

⟦ REASONABLE ACCOMMODATION ⟧

Reasonable accommodation is any change or adjustment to a job or work environment that permits a qualified applicant or employee with a disability to participate in the job application process, perform the essential functions of a job, or enjoy benefits and privileges of employment equal to those of other employees.

Types of accommodations include:

• Providing or modifying equipment, that is, the *how*, such as a golf cart or a telecommunications device for the deaf (TDD)

• Adjusting a work schedule, that is, the *when*

• Job restructuring (focusing on essential functions) or reassignment

• Adjusting or modifying examinations, training materials, or policies

• Reassigning or retraining other employees to do the marginal tasks

• Making the workplace readily accessible and usable by people with disabilities

That last type of accomodation has been the most visible and expensive impact of the ADA (not just Title I). It includes ramps, designated disability parking, restructured restrooms, and so on. But most Title I accommodations are surprisingly easy and low cost, and well worth the investment: 31 percent cost nothing, such as rearranging furniture for someone in a wheelchair; and 88 percent cost under $1,000. For example, a TDD costs $150–$200.

Note: An employer is not required to provide personal aids, such as a guide dog or wheelchair, but must allow them to be used in the workplace.

Notice, however, that most of the types of accommodation listed above relate to employment practices, not equipment.

We now draw your attention particularly to modifying policies. We know of at least one employer who ran afoul of ADA by inflexibly applying its (basically sound) medical leave policy.

How do you determine what accommodation is needed? There are many government and nonprofit agency resources available to assist you. (See the Resource Guide.) Start with your in-house expert, that is, collaborate with the employee with the disability. And don't be afraid to experiment. The accommodation chosen need not be the most expensive or the employee's first choice. It simply needs to enable the employee to perform the essential functions of the job.

An employer is not required to provide an accommodation that would be an undue hardship to the organization, that is, would require significant difficulty or expense. Be prepared to justify this! And bear in mind that outside funding or payment plans often are available, and the employee may choose to pay for some of the cost as well.

YOUR RESPONSIBILITIES AS A WORKPLACE LEADER

1. *Provide equal access* to the benefits and privileges of employment. For example:
   - Health insurance, cafeteria, lounges, parking, transportation, and so on
   - Training—this may require communications-related accommodation

- Career opportunities, such as promotion, transfer, special assignments, and so on

2. **Ensure no harassment or discrimination.** Harassing someone because of a disability is just as serious as harassing someone because of race, sex, or religion. See Tool #19 for harassment prevention guidelines.

3. **Job descriptions** are significantly impacted by the ADA. They must:
   - Be thorough and accurate
   - Be based on fact, that is, actually performed on the job, not a wish list
   - Be current and flexible, that is, kept up to date
   - Distinguish essential from marginal functions
   - Focus on what is to be done, rather than when or how
   - Be used when making all employment decisions, such as hiring, promotion, disciplinary action, and ...

4. **Performance evaluations** during which:
   - You should focus on performance of essential job functions, based on job description.
   - You should ignore the disability or any accommodations that may have been made when evaluating performance. (Although you may talk about accommodations as part of a discussion of future goals and action plans.)
   - You are prohibited from asking an employee about his or her disability and the accommodation needed, unless it is visible or the employee brings it to your attention.

THE HIRING PROCESS

There are many ADA-related issues involved with the hiring process.

Access and Accommodation

Employers must ensure that there is equal access to the employment office and to job notifications and provide alternative methods of completing application forms, interviews, and testing that accommodate disabilities.

Applications and Interviews

Focus on ability. You *may* ask applicants about:

- Necessary experience, education, training, and skills
- Whether they can satisfy the essential job requirements
- How much time they took off in previous jobs, but not why
- The reason they left previous jobs
- Any past discipline received

You *may* ask applicants to describe or demonstrate how they will perform the essential duties of the job, *if* you ask this of all applicants or *if* the disability is visible or is brought to your attention by the applicant.

Avoid medical or disability-related questions. You *may not* ask applicants about:

- A physical or mental impairment
- How the disability occurred ← watch out for this one; it is a tempting icebreaker
- Use of medication
- Workers' compensation history

If the disability is obvious (e.g., blindness, deafness, or being in a wheelchair), you may ask if accommodation is needed.

Testing

Physical agility, manual dexterity, or mental acuity tests are allowed if required of all applicants (for similar positions). The tests must be clearly job related and measure *what* needs to be done (with accommodation made for how and when).

Preemployment drug testing (for illegal substances) also is permitted.

Medical Exams and History

These may be conducted only *after* a job offer, but can be before starting work. The offer may be made contingent on passing the medical exam, if only job-related factors are used and this is required of all applicants.

The diagnosis must be kept confidential. Only release symptoms to health/safety personnel (for example,) and the impact on job performance to those with a need to know, such as the hiring manager. Medical records must be filed separately from the personnel file, for example, in the health/safety office.

Safety-Related Concerns

You are allowed to not hire an applicant—or to terminate a current employee—who poses a direct threat that cannot be eliminated or sufficiently reduced through reasonable accommodation. *Direct threat* is defined as a significant risk of substantial harm to the health or safety of the individual or others. It cannot be a slightly increased risk or speculation about future risk. And it must be based on evidence, not generalized fear.

EVERYONE'S RESPONSIBILITIES

Self-Identification

If an employee thinks he or she will need a reasonable accommodation in order to participate in the application process or perform essential job functions (or enjoy its benefits and privileges), it is the employee's responsibility to inform you that an accommodation will be needed.

Employers are required to provide reasonable accommodation only for the disability limitations of which they are aware. In fact, you are prohibited from asking employees about their disability and the accommodation they may need unless the disability is visible or they bring it to your attention.

Note: The aforementioned should be communicated to your applicants and employees.

Suggesting and Implementing Accommodations

Your employees should be instructed to collaborate with you in suggesting and implementing accommodations, whether it is bringing a guide dog into the workplace, use of a TDD, or simply being able to reach file cabinets. Individuals with disabilities probably know better than anyone else what will enable them to do the job.

We recommend that you discuss the intended accommodation with your HR and/or health services department prior to implementation.

Working with People with Disabilities

Many of us have limited experience interacting with people with various disabilities. We want to do the right thing but may feel a bit awkward and unsure.

To help you get started, we highly recommend the award-winning video *The 10 Commandments of Communicating with People with Disabilities*. It puts a human face on the issues we've been discussing in this tool. Reprinted here are the commandments from that video:

The 10 Commandments of Communicating with People with Disabilities

I.   Speak *directly* to the person, rather than through an interpreter.

II.   Always offer to *shake hands* when introduced.

III.   Always *identify yourself* and others with you when meeting someone who is blind.

IV.   If you offer assistance, *wait* until the offer is accepted. Listen, wait, or ask for instructions.

V.   Treat adults *as adults*.

VI.   Do not *lean against* or hang on someone's wheelchair or cart. They treat their chair as extensions of their bodies.

VII.   *Listen* attentively when talking with people who have difficulty speaking…and wait for them to finish.

VIII. Place yourself at *eye level* when speaking with someone in a wheelchair or on crutches.

IX.   *Tap* a person who's deaf *on the shoulder* or *wave your hand* to get his or her attention.

X.   *Relax*…don't be embarrassed if you use common expressions that seem to relate to a person's disability.

Adapted from many sources as a public service by United Cerebral Palsy Associates, Inc. (UCPA) and by Irene M. Ward & Associates (Columbus, Ohio), also as a public service. Copyright 1994, Irene M. Ward & Associates.

3

Leader Effectiveness

OPEN TWO-WAY COMMUNICATION

Part 1 presented principles and techniques to *influence* today's employees—to motivate, energize, and retain them. You learned that employees want to feel appreciated and listened to, be involved and informed, and learn and grow. That is, they want (and need) open two-way communication with their leaders, especially with their immediate boss.

This part shows you *how* to do it. You will learn the core skills entailed with two-way communication in the workplace: feedback, inquiry, and active listening—skills that you will also apply in Part 4 to guide your employees and optimize their performance.

In Tool #7, you'll learn how and why to give feedback—both positive and constructive. We explain what feedback is (and is not), teach you when and how to deliver each type of feedback and how to combine both types, and provide opportunities to begin applying this skill with your own employees.

Tool #8 unlocks the other side of the two-way communication coin: inquiry to solicit your employees' ideas and opinions, and active listening to ensure that you hear them and that they feel heard. We discuss why inquiry and active listening are so important (but are underutilized), give you an opportunity to assess your current effectiveness, teach you how to inquire and listen, and launch you on activities to practice these skills.

TOOL SEVEN

Tell Them What Worked ... and What Didn't

FEEDBACK

What is feedback? It's simply information given to and received by people regarding their behavior. Notice: behavior, not character.

Feedback is a continuous and interactive process, best given as close to the time of the behavior as possible. Do not wait until an annual performance review; instead, frequently have a two-way communication with employees regarding their performance and interactions with others.

Feedback can be positive or constructive. Constructive? You might think of this as negative, but, as you will see, constructive feedback is a lot more than that.

Why is feedback needed? It's difficult for us to see ourselves objectively, especially the impact our behavior has on other people or on complex systems, for example, the operations of an enterprise. And it is impossible to see ourselves as others see us...without feedback.

Think of feedback as a mirror that another person holds up for us to look into. The best mirrors are those without distortion (such as the biases or hidden agendas of the person providing the feedback), untarnished by either animosity or fondness.

—————[**POSITIVE FEEDBACK...**   ]——————
                    aka PRAISE

Why should we give positive feedback?

Among other reasons, remember that more than anything else, employees want to be appreciated for their work. Unfortunately, most of us are criticized four times more than we're praised. We need to reverse that!

Here's how to do it:

1. Start by describing the *behavior* (not the person) using specific language and examples. (Over the years, as we have coached managers on feedback, lack of specificity is the major weakness we have observed.)

2. Then describe the *impact* of the behavior. What positive consequences does it have? Why are you praising the person for it?

3. And show *appreciation* for the person's effort. This can be as simple as saying "Thanks!"

Be sincere, not manipulative. Your goal is to catch people doing something right and make them aware of it. The goal is not to get them to work harder—although they probably will.

Here's a simple example:

"I appreciate your working late last night to finish the BoolaBoola project." ← **behavior**

"You helped us to meet our deadline, and that helps keep our customers satisfied." ← **impact** (short-term and broader context)

"Thanks for the extra effort!" ← **appreciation** (also shown in the opening statement)

> Use **positive** feedback to *reinforce* appropriate,
> productive, desirable behavior ... and
> to show *appreciation*.

APPLICATION #1

1. *Identify* someone from work who deserves positive feedback.

2. *Write* what you would say to this person, using the behavior–impact–appreciation guidelines.

3. *Give* that person the feedback, that is, say it to the person.

4. *Don't worry* if you feel a bit awkward the first couple of times that you do this; it's just like learning any new skill.

—[**CONSTRUCTIVE FEEDBACK**]—

Just as employees need to hear from you about what they are doing right, they also need your observations about what they are doing that isn't yet quite right.

The first thing to know about constructive feedback is that it is not criticizing or reprimanding.

One of the best-known books on managing people is *The One-Minute Manager* by Blanchard and Johnson (2000). In their book, they talk about a one-minute praising (very similar to the positive feedback previously described) and a one-minute reprimand.

But we don't think that "reprimand" is the appropriate word. Short of illegal or clearly immoral acts, none of us deserves to be reprimanded. Instead, what we deserve, and need, is to be redirected toward different, more effective behavior. We urge you to think of constructive feedback as a one-minute (or longer) *redirect*.

Why should we give constructive feedback? Among other reasons, remember what zaps employee motivation (see Tool #1)—unclear expectations, withholding information, and criticism. Constructive feedback *clarifies* expectations, *provides* information, and when done correctly, is *not* criticism.

Use constructive feedback to discourage inappropriate, unproductive, and undesirable behaviors.

Thus far, this parallels positive feedback. If that were all that construc-tive feedback did, you could conceivably call it negative. But constructive feedback does something more; it also guides the individual toward more effective behaviors.

Here's how to do it:

1. First, describe the specific, observable behavior using facts—just like positive feedback. Vague generalities and unsubstantiated opinion are useless in improving performance.

    Avoid judgments and evaluations. Describe the behavior, not the person. This is not a character assessment and certainly not a char-acter assassination.

2. Next, describe the *impact* of the behavior, why you are bringing it to the employee's attention. It's the same as with positive feedback, but this time the impact is undesirable or short of optimum.

3. Then check for the individual's understanding of your feedback and ask for input—*inquiry*. This step is unique to constructive feedback. It is usually not needed in positive feed-back. (We'll say more about how to do this in Tool #8.)

4. Finally, suggest an alternative by describing the desired behavior. That is, your *expectation*—which takes the place of the apprecia-tion that you expressed in positive feedback.

We say finally, but in practice, you may very well go back and forth between these last two steps—continually checking for understanding and soliciting the employee's ideas as you talk about the desired behavior.

Here's a simple example:

"When you return 15 minutes late from lunch... ← **behavior**

...others have to cover your job." ← **impact**

"Do you see why we need you back on time?" ← **inquiry**

"I'd like you to be back at your workstation at 1:00, ready to go."
← **expectation**

"What needs to happen to make that possible?" ← **inquiry**

Use **constructive** feedback to **_discourage_**
inappropriate, unproductive, undesirable behaviors ... and
to **_guide_** the individual toward effective behaviors.

APPLICATION #2

1. _Identify_ someone from work who needs constructive feedback.

2. _Write_ what you would actually say to this person, using the behavior–impact–inquiry–expectation guidelines.

3. _Give_ that person the feedback, that is, _say_ it to the person...and _listen_ to what the person says in response to your inquiries.

4. _Don't worry_ if you feel a bit awkward the first couple of times that you do this, it's just like learning any new skill.

COMBINING POSITIVE AND CONSTRUCTIVE FEEDBACK

Even if you avoid criticizing and give constructive feedback in the most benevolent way, it's not as much fun for the employee as receiving positive feedback. So, it might be helpful to:

1. Begin the session with positive feedback.
2. Next, give the constructive feedback.
3. End the conversation with more positive feedback.

What do you think this method is called? The Sandwich Technique. That is, the constructive feedback is sandwiched between two layers of positive feedback.

If you choose to use the Sandwich Technique, be careful with your transition from positive to constructive feedback. Avoid words like _but_ or _however_. Why do you think we say that? _But_ or _however_ tends to undercut the sincerity (and the desired feel-good impact) of your positive feedback. Instead, end the positive statement with a period. And begin a new sentence with the constructive feedback. Or use phrases like, *To improve on this…What concerns me is…At the same time…*

What might be a potential disadvantage to the Sandwich Technique? Well, if you always precede constructive feedback with positive feedback, whenever you simply want to give positive feedback, your employees will be waiting in fear for the other shoe to drop!

What we prefer is the Open Sandwich. That is:

1. Start right out with the constructive feedback. (Remember, you're not bawling them out. You don't need to cushion the blow.)
2. Then, finish off the conversation with positive feedback.

The closing positive feedback puts the redirect into the perspective of the employee's overall performance. In effect, what you're communicating is: You are a good (or great) employee. Of course you are not perfect. None of us is.

For example:

INITIAL CONSTRUCTIVE FEEDBACK

"When you accomplish all the tasks yourself…" ← **behavior**

"…your coworkers feel excluded and don't learn." ← **impact**

"Does that make sense to you?" ← **inquiry**

"I'd like you to involve your teammates in some of the tasks in your project." ← **expectation**

"What are some tasks you could get others to work on?" ← **inquiry**

CLOSING POSITIVE FEEDBACK

"Your willingness to accomplish so much…" ← **behavior**

"…is a real asset to this team and will serve you well in your career." ← **impact**

"I'm really glad to have you on the team. Thanks for all your hard work!"
← **appreciation**

Do not use either version of the Sandwich Technique, however, if you do not regard the employee as at least fairly good overall, if, for example, you're on the verge of firing the individual.

APPLICATION #3

1. *Identify* a good employee who could use some constructive feedback.

2. *Write* what you would say in the initial constructive feedback, using the behavior–impact–inquiry–expectation guidelines.

3. *Write* what you would say in the closing positive feedback, using the behavior–impact–appreciation guidelines.

4. *Give* that person the feedback, that is, *say* it to the person...*listen* to what he or she says in response to your inquiries and gauge how the person feels about both aspects of the feedback.

5. *Don't worry* if you feel a bit awkward the first couple of times that you do this; it's just like learning any new skill.

⎡ CONSTRUCTIVE FEEDBACK IS NOT... ⎤

Constructive feedback is often confused with two other interpersonal communications. The first is *anger*. If an employee has done something contrary to your expectations, you may very well feel some degree of anger or annoyance. What can we say about anger?

- Anger is neither good nor bad. If you feel it, you feel it.
- Allow yourself to experience your anger fully, maybe even express it. (See Tool #17.)
- But expressing anger is not feedback.
- Do not let your anger pollute the feedback process!

Constructive feedback also can be confused with *assertion:*

- Asserting yourself is good, that is, if it's assertion, *not* aggression. (See Tool #16.)

- Assertion has some elements in common with feedback, but there are important differences:

     The focus of assertion is *your* wants and needs.

     The focus of feedback is the *other* person's behavior.

8

TOOL EIGHT

Ask Them...Then Listen

The other side of the two-way communication coin is *inquiry* to solicit your employees' ideas and opinions and *active listening* to ensure that you hear them and that they feel heard.

INQUIRY

What is inquiry? It is the opposite of telling or advocating. You ask for a person's ideas or input in a nonjudgmental way. By tone of voice and reputation, the person needs to be assured that whatever ideas or opinions are expressed will be okay.

You withhold telling what you think and avoid arguing your own point of view—very difficult for many of us! You just inquire...and then listen to what the person has to say. Inquiry really is very simple, although not necessarily easy. You merely ask, "What do you think?"

Why do you think inquiry is needed? Because this is a book, rather than a face-to-face dialogue, we can't avoid violating inquiry guidelines to *tell* you:

1. Inquiry can be used to confirm understanding, for example, as part of the constructive feedback process. (See Tool #7.)

2. Most employees probably know their jobs better than anyone else. They are your in-house experts for a great many issues, including their own performance improvement and development needs.

3. Inquiry gets the person involved and participating. Remember that employees really want to feel in on things.

4. Inquiry helps build buy-in and commitment. Is gaining the commitment of your employees ever a challenge for you?

5. Inquiry helps build a person's self-esteem. Requesting a person's ideas and opinions implies that his or her thoughts are important, that the person is important. Inquiry validates the employee as someone who really matters in your workplace.

Considering all the positive outcomes of inquiry, it's surprising that most managers do not engage in it that much.

How do you do it? Whenever you face a problem or task—not just during constructive feedback—ask for input from the persons involved. Ask what they think should be done. If necessary, get them to open up by probing their prior experiences and perspectives.

So what do you do if their ideas are not workable? Look for parts of the idea to build on or, at a minimum, credit the person for the idea and explain why you cannot use it.

> Use **inquiry** to *confirm* understanding,
> get *input*, and *build* commitment.

ACTIVE LISTENING

Inquiry and listening go hand in hand. If you don't really listen to what the other person has to say in response to your inquiry, you deny yourself and the person of all the potential positive outcomes.

Really listening is not a passive process. You need to actively engage with the other person.

To gauge how actively you listen, you may want to complete this Active Listening Self-Assessment.

Worksheet 8-1. Active Listening Self-Assessment.

Recall an instance when you were listening to a request (or complaint) made or instructions given by an employee, customer, or boss. Visualize the situation as clearly as possible. With that in mind, indicate with a check mark the degree to which each of the following statements accurately describes your behavior:

	Not Really	Somewhat	Definitely
1. I made regular eye contact with the speaker.			
2. I asked questions for clarification.			
3. I showed concern by acknowledging feelings.			
4. I restated or paraphrased some of his or her words.			
5. I sought first to understand, then to be understood.			
6. I was relaxed and emotionally calm.			
7. I reacted nonverbally (e.g., smile, nod, frown, touch).			
8. I paid close attention and did not let my mind wander.			
9. I did not change the subject without warning.			
10. I acted appropriately on what was said.			
11. I interrupted often.			
12. I made up my mind while he or she was still speaking.			
13. I finished many of his or her sentences.			
14. I gave quick advice, even if it was not requested.			
15. I was impatient.			
16. I thought about my replies while he or she was speaking.			

Adapted from *The Business of Listening,* by Diane Bone, Axzo Press/Crisp, 1994.

Now step back and look at the pattern of your check marks for the first ten statements and for the last six statements. Are most of your check marks for the first ten in the Definitely column...and, for the last six, in the Not Really column? If so (and you were candid), you already are a very active listener. To become even better, think about any items you checked in the other two columns for both groupings and consciously work to improve the behavior(s) described.

Or, were most of your check marks for the first ten statements in the Not Really and Somewhat columns...and in the Definitely column for the last six? If so, there is definitely room for improvement. You cannot really describe yourself as an active listener.

And notice the overall style of your listening:

- Are you very participative (asking questions, paraphrasing, reacting nonverbally, etc.), but intrusive (interrupting, finishing sentences, giving advice, etc.)? → Try pulling back a bit. Remember what we said about inquiry: Withhold telling what you think.

- Are you not fully focused on what the person is saying (e.g., no eye contact, letting your mind wander, thinking about your replies)? → Try putting other issues to the side and give the person your complete attention.

- Are you a passive listener (e.g., not asking questions, not paraphrasing, not showing concern, etc.)? → Try to interact more with the other person.

THE CHALLENGE OF ACTIVE LISTENING

Most people are not very good listeners. Why is that? There are three underlying reasons:

1. We are all pretty busy juggling myriad priorities in our work and personal lives

2. These priorities engage a great deal of our attention and it's a challenge to put them to the side and focus fully on another person's issues. Because of this, we tend to take shortcuts—leaping to conclusions and assumptions—based on insufficient information.

3. Active listening is a learned skill, in which most people have had little or no training.

SIX ELEMENTS OF ACTIVE LISTENING

The following list breaks down the process of active listening:

1. *Stop* what you are doing and give the person your full attention.

2. Use *silence* and do not complete the other person's sentences.

3. Collect the *facts* on the issue at hand.

4. Then go deeper. Listen to what is *really* being said. What does the person want you to understand?

5. Use *reflective* questioning, that is, paraphrase/restate comments to get confirmation:

   "Let me see if I understand you. Are you saying…?"

   "You want…Is that right?"

6. Ask *clarifying* and open-ended questions to inquire:

   "Give me an example."

   "What would you like to see happen?"

   "Anything else?"…"Tell me more."

If what the other person is saying is very simple and has little emotional content, you may need to apply only the first two elements, in other words, *shut up and listen*, although adding a reflective question at the end is always a good idea. For example, "You need to leave work a half-hour early today for personal business and will make up that time by coming in a half-hour early tomorrow. Right? Okay!"

However, for anything more complex, and especially if there are emotions involved (as in a complaint or a personal problem), you will definitely want to apply all six elements.

APPLICATION

1. *Pair off* with another person who wants to improve listening skills.

2. One of you plays an upset person; the other plays the listener.

3. *Upset* person:

    Choose one of the following situations…or

    Remember a time you were angry or upset.

    Explain the situation to the listener…and then *act* it out.

4. *Listener:* Apply the six elements of active listening. Be there for the person.

5. *Switch* roles and repeat Steps #3 and #4.

6. *Talk* (and listen) to each other about the experience.

SITUATION #1: THE DEMANDING SUPERVISOR

Your supervisor has been making unrealistic demands (e.g., absurd deadlines) and has been verbally abusive when the demands are not met. You've had it up to here! Nothing you do is right.

SITUATION #2: THE DENIED INSURANCE CLAIM

Your health insurance provider has denied your medical insurance claim. It was for a somewhat unusual procedure to treat a serious condition of your child/spouse/self. (Select whichever is applicable to you.) You, and your doctor, regard the procedure as absolutely necessary. You are furious!

SITUATION #3: THE WORK/LIFE CRISIS

Occasionally, you need to take time off, come in late, or leave a bit early in order to take care of personal business (e.g., child care, if applicable to you). Every time you do, your supervisor gives you a hard time. And now, he or she has given you a written warning about it. It's unfair! You feel angry and frightened (you need to keep your job and you need to deal with these personal issues).

PART FOUR

Optimizing Contributions

THE THREE STRATEGIES...AND
A PRECURSOR

In the introduction to this book, we defined leader as a person who guides and influences people to willingly follow a chosen direction: the vision and mission.

Part 1 dealt with influencing employees to willingly follow your lead toward the vision. This part unlocks how to *guide* your employees to effectively accomplish your organization's mission, that is, how to optimize their contributions.

This entails three different strategies:

1. Coaching marginal or good employees to become good or great employees

2. Mentoring great employees to advance

3. Team building for employees as a group

Part 3 covered some of the skills needed to execute these strategies. Now you will learn how to apply those skills—as well as a few others—in order to optimize your employees' contributions.

Tool #9 describes how to diagnose performance problems, which is a necessary precursor to any form of intervention, for example, coaching.

In Tool #10, you will learn how to coach marginal employees to improve their performance…and coach good employees to become even better.

Tool #11 unlocks how to mentor your already great employees to further grow and advance.

Tool #12 looks at your employees as a group and reveals how to optimize the groups' performance and, perhaps, transform it into a real or even high-performance team.

Diagnose Problems

Have you ever had to supervise a problem employee?

When asked in our training sessions, this question elicits a nodding of heads, usually accompanied by rueful chuckles. All too often, when dealing with an employee whose performance or behavior does not meet expectations, we attribute the problems to some flaw in the person's character—labeling the individual a "problem" employee. Such attribution and labeling usually is unfair and unwarranted...and is always counterproductive.

Although there are exceptions...

> The *true* cause of most performance problems
> has nothing to do with an employee's character.

Once you grasp this **Secret,** you open yourself to diagnosing...

THE FIVE ROOT CAUSES OF PERFORMANCE PROBLEMS

The real cause of most problems falls into one or more of the following five categories:

1. **Expectations.** Does the employee know what is expected? Does the employee even know there is a problem?

    These both may be obvious to you, but often they are not to the employee. (This is a classic symptom of not receiving constructive feedback, described in Tool #7.)

2. **Training and Ability.** Does the employee have the requisite skills, abilities, and aptitudes to perform the task?

    If he or she does not have the aptitudes, you may need to reassign or fire the employee. But if it's a skills/abilities issue, you then need to ask yourself...

    Has the employee received the appropriate training to perform the task? This may include formal classroom training or education. Even more likely, however, is the need for on-the-job training (OJT), that is, to show the employee how to do it.

3. **Job Design.** Does the employee have the necessary tools and resources to perform the task?

    Those resources include not only physical tools but also convenient and timely access to information and to you, the manager.

    Does the system support good performance? This gets into such issues as communications, scheduling, and teamwork, within a department and between departments.

4. **Work Environment.** This refers not only to the physical environment but also to how employees are treated.

    Is good performance rewarded or punished? For example, is there an informal standard set by peer pressure to not work too efficiently? Or are you assigning extra, more demanding tasks to your best employees without rewarding them appropriately?

    Is poor performance rewarded? That is, do you tolerate it? Do you treat your marginal employees the same as you treat your outstanding ones? → Hey, why not goof off?

    Is the employee being treated fairly? Not only in your eyes, but also in theirs. This includes:

    • Discrimination and harassment (See Tool #19.)

    • Sensitivity to differences (See all of Part 2.)

- Equity theory (See Tip #1 of Tool #1.)

- Favoritism (See Principle #2 of Tool #3.)

5. **Personal/Motivational Problem.** Does a problem exist in the employee's personal life that may contribute to poor performance? (See Tool #3.) For example, a frequent reason for lateness and attendance problems is parental responsibilities.

Or is the employee's morale or attitude preventing the employee from successfully applying his or her skills and abilities? (See Tools #1 and #15.) This may or may not be subject to your control or influence, but it's certainly worth looking into. Low morale or even a negative attitude may be a symptom of excessive job demands, (See Tool #2.) or not receiving deserved positive feedback. (See Tool #7.)

DIAGNOSIS

Prior to taking action on a performance problem (e.g., coaching or giving constructive feedback), you need to think about the five categories of potential root causes, asking yourself each of the questions. You probably won't be able to answer all of them without consulting someone else. So ask your in-house expert—the employee!

You may find that it is not a performance intervention that is called for, but a change in the system or in your own behavior.

Note: Although critical for addressing performance problems, such diagnoses can also be useful when assisting good employees to develop into great employees.

APPLICATION

1. *Identify* one of your employees who needs performance improvement.

2. *Describe* that person's performance problems (i.e., the symptoms, not the causes).

3. *Ask* yourself each question in the five categories as it pertains to the problems. Answer as best as you can.

4. *Determine* those questions for which you need additional information, for example, from the employee and/or others.

5. Ask *them.*

10

Coach the Good Ones…and the Not So Good

Coaching is the first of three strategies we present to optimize employee contributions. It brings together all of the skills addressed in previous tools as a cohesive process to improve or enhance the performance of both marginal and good employees.

Although the process is essentially the same and the same skill set is utilized, it is helpful to distinguish two categories of coaching, based on the type of employee to be coached:

1. Performance problem coaching for marginal employees
2. Development coaching for good employees

Note: If you're curious about what to do for your great employees, see the next tool.

PERFORMANCE PROBLEM COACHING

Performance problem coaching is used with an employee whose performance or behavior is not meeting expectations. The purpose is to correct problems so that the employee meets standards or expectations.

Performance problem coaching helps a
marginal employee become a ***good*** employee.

Use performance problem coaching whenever:

- An employee's quality or productivity does not meet expectations
- An employee's behavior interferes with his or her performance
- An employee's behavior interferes with the performance of others
- An employee violates a policy or procedure

Which of your employees need performance problem coaching?

DEVELOPMENT COACHING

Development coaching is used to further develop employees whose overall performance already meets expectations. The purpose is to maximize an employee's performance in the current job.

Development coaching usually is less intense or emotionally demanding than performance problem coaching, because the stakes are not as high, that is, the employee's continued employment is not in question.

Development coaching helps a *good* employee
become a ***great*** employee.

Use development coaching to:

- Add new skills or hone existing skills
- Help the employee apply knowledge or skills to the job
- Enhance performance so the employee works more effectively
- Prepare for an upcoming project or assignment
- Help the employee solve problems

Which of your employees need development coaching?

FOUR STEPS OF A COACHING OR MENTORING DIALOGUE

Whether you will be conducting performance problem or development coaching (or the mentoring discussed in the next tool), you'll be doing it in the form of a conversation.

To be most effective, there are four steps:

1. *Set the* **purpose** *of the meeting.* Describe what you want to discuss and why. Seek the employees' involvement in the meeting—why it is in their self-interest to actively participate.

2. *Gather and clarify* **information** *to define the situation.* Use inquiry to gain information. Offer your ideas (e.g., provide feedback), as necessary. Apply the diagnosis process described in the previous tool.

3. *Identify and develop* **ideas** *to address the situation.* Use inquiry to solicit ideas, offer your ideas, and discuss and develop best ideas.

4. *Determine an* **action plan.** Agree on action steps that are clear, measurable, achievable, and have target dates, and on a plan to monitor progress. Offer encouragement and support.

Many of the skills covered in Part 3 are referenced in these steps. The other skill from that part—active listening—is utilized throughout the process.

Each of these four steps, and their components, is important. Eliminating or abbreviating any of them will undermine the others and the effectiveness of the entire process.

In Steps #2 and #3, the balance between inquiry and offering your ideas (e.g., feedback) depends on the nature and severity of the performance problem or development need, and on the results of your initial diagnosis of root causes. (See Tool #9.) For example, if you believe the employee has a positive attitude, but does not know there is a problem, you probably want to emphasize feedback during Step #2 and inquiry during Step #3. On the other hand, if you have previously made the employee aware of the performance problems, but the person has shown little improvement, you may want to emphasize inquiry in Step #2 (i.e., get the employee to acknowledge the problem), but be moderately directive in Steps #3 and #4.

Do not shortchange the final point in Step #4! If we had to choose from among inquiry, feedback, action planning, and encouragement only one technique to improve performance, we would choose encouragement. People with high morale who believe that the boss knows they can do it, are more likely to find their own way and succeed than those who are clear on the end result expected, but doubt their ability to achieve it.

———{   **TWO COACHING SCENARIOS**   }———

The following scenarios provide an opportunity to test your understanding of the coaching process and to practice applying what you learned in this and the previous tool, as well as the skills from Part 3.

We start with an example of coaching to address a development need of a good employee:

DEVELOPMENT COACHING SCENARIO: PRODUCTIVE PAT

Productive Pat is one of your best employees and has consistently been a superior performer in terms of quality and quantity of work. You rely heavily on Pat to solve problems quickly and to help you take a different look at projects and issues in your department. Whenever you want to make sure all of the potential problems in a project or ideas are identified and assessed, you turn to Pat.

Pat typically gets along well with her coworkers in carrying out the day-to-day, routine duties of the job. Problems arise, however, when Pat has to work with others to get new projects started or problems solved. She can visualize where things need to get to before the majority of her coworkers do. Too often, however, Pat loses patience with them.

She has made it abundantly clear to you that waiting for others to catch up and to buy in (which she calls "playing politics") is a conspicuous waste of time. Pat has said more than once that she wishes we could all cut to the chase and get the job done.

Coworkers confirm Pat's strengths. Whenever they need a reliable, knowledgeable person for a special project, Pat is their first choice. As long as it remains one-on-one, the process moves very smoothly.

But when the project requires Pat to get input from others, to build cooperation to share responsibility, to move slowly until everyone understands and agrees to the process, Pat grows impatient. She issues orders and charges ahead without seeking ideas or approval from others. She does not "see the value of revisiting and re-presenting the same stuff over and over in order to build something as stupid as consensus." Frankly, Pat needs to develop these skills in her current job before she becomes eligible for promotion.

Pat has told you that she wants to know what she must do to move up to the next level in the organization. She certainly possesses the expertise, but her style and lack of patience have rubbed a number of others, including your boss, the wrong way. To enable Pat to grow in her present role, you need to help her develop the art of "politics."

Think about how you would prepare for and conduct the coaching session as Pat's supervisor. You need to address:

1. What do you want to *accomplish* in this meeting?
2. What are some *concerns* that you need to address?
3. How will you give *feedback* (positive and constructive) so Pat knows she needs to improve her interpersonal and influence skills and that you appreciate her strengths?
4. How will you use *inquiry* to gain Pat's involvement and commitment?
5. How do you expect to use *active listening* during the meeting?
6. How will you provide *encouragement* and support?

Next, we present a more challenging example of coaching to address the performance problems of a marginal, albeit talented, employee:

PERFORMANCE PROBLEM COACHING SCENARIO: ROCKIN' ROBIN

Rockin' Robin is an affable employee who, at times, produces great quantities of creative work. However, Robin's good qualities are offset by habitual tardiness, inattention to detail, and often missed deadlines—all of which is frustrating to you and resented by Robin's coworkers.

Robin feels his good personality and moments of great creativity (for which he expects extraordinary praise) make up for any deficiencies, which he tends to minimize. And whenever Robin's lateness, inaccuracies, or missed deadlines are commented on (by you, Robin's manager, or by coworkers), he becomes defensive.

Recently you notice that Robin looks glassy-eyed in the mornings when he eventually arrives. His defensiveness now verges on hostility.

What's going on? Is Robin using drugs? Drinking heavily? One thing you are sure of: Robin's behavior and performance deficiencies can no longer be tolerated. At the same time, however, you'd hate to lose him. In some ways he's your best employee.

Think about how you would prepare for and conduct the coaching session as Robin's supervisor. You need to address:

1. What do you want to *accomplish* in this meeting?

2. What are the possible *cause(s)* for the problem? (See Tool #9.)

3. How do you get past Robin's *defensiveness*?

4. How will you give *feedback* (positive and constructive) so that Robin knows he must address these serious issues and that you appreciate his strengths?

5. How will you use *inquiry* to clarify causes and encourage Robin's participation in the meeting?

6. How do you expect to use *active listening* during the meeting?

7. How will you provide *encouragement* and support?

Note: Be cautious in talking about Robin's attitude. A discussion about attitude can create defensiveness. Avoid using the word *attitude* and, instead, focus on observable behaviors. (Tool #15 is devoted entirely to attitude. It is a very real and important human attribute—for the individual. But it is best not to be commented on by others.)

—[**FOUR TIPS FOR PERFORMANCE PROBLEM COACHING**]—

1. Address problems *early*. Nip them in the bud, so to speak.

2. Be a problem-solving *ally*, not an adversary. People move toward and with their allies, but fight or flee from their adversaries.

3. *Involve* the employee as much as possible in the process. It is that individual's job or career that is on the line.

4. If the problem *persists*, document your actions, keep your manager informed, and work with your HR department to take further action (e.g., the steps entailed in your organization's progressive disciplinary policy, up through termination).

APPLICATION

1. *Select* one employee you identified earlier in this tool who needs coaching—either for development or performance problems.

2. Sketch out a *script* for a coaching session. (Refer to the Four Steps of a Coaching or Mentoring Dialogue.)

3. Be sure you are able to answer the *questions* posed in the two scenarios just presented.

4. Go ahead and actually *coach* that employee.

Mentor the Great Ones

Mentoring is the strategy used with an employee whose performance exceeds expectations and therefore is ready for new opportunities. The purpose of mentoring is to groom and guide an employee to assume additional responsibilities and/or advance in his or her career.

Mentoring involves sharing your knowledge and experience to help an employee create and fulfill a career plan.

Mentoring helps a *great* employee grow and advance.

Use mentoring whenever:

- An employee's performance exceeds expectations and the person is ready for advancement or new opportunities.
- An employee seeks career-related advice.
- Management or other relevant positions need to be filled.

Note: The term *mentor* often is used to describe someone other than the employee's supervisor who guides the employee in making career decisions and taking career steps. This tool can be helpful to someone in that role. However, here it is geared specifically to those in a supervisory role who take on this responsibility with regard to their direct reports.

Which of your employees need mentoring?

Tips for Mentoring

1. *Inquire* into your employees' career desires and frustrations. Do not make assumptions! For example, not all outstanding employees want to be managers.

2. Whatever their aspirations, *offer* the developmental assignments, training, networking, and personal/professional contacts that will aid in fulfilling those goals.

3. *Do not* make promises about promotions or future jobs. Instead, talk about possibilities.

4. *Coordinate* your efforts with senior management. Employees' careers may take them into areas that are outside your direct control.

—[THE MENTORING PREP SHEET]—

A mentoring session follows the same four steps as the coaching and mentoring dialogue covered in Tool #10, and the same skill set from Part 3 is applied. The content and emotional dynamics of the session, however, are quite different.

Instead of correcting a performance problem or addressing a development need in the current job, your focus now is the employee's career and, potentially, helping the person to prepare for another job.

Completing the following Mentoring Prep Sheet prior to meeting with the employee can help guide you and the employee during your discussions:

Worksheet 11-1. Mentoring Prep Sheet.

_____

Name of employee

1. What do you *think* are this employees' *career aspirations?*

_____

_____

2. Based on these aspirations (that you will *confirm* with inquiry), what position(s) in your organization should be the *next step* in this person's career?

_____

_____

3. From an organizational perspective, *how likely* is this opportunity? *When?*

_____

_____

4. What *personal* barriers (e.g., behavioral, family, relocation, etc.) might prevent this?

_____

_____

5. What do you and the employee *need to do* to prepare for this position?

_____

_____

- Task/project *assignments* _____
- Skills or behavioral *coaching* _____
- *Exposure*/visibility _____
- *Networking* _____
- In-house *training*/certification _____
- *External* training/certification _____
- Formal *education* _____

6. *With whom* do you need to discuss, confirm, and coordinate this?

_____

_____

—[**OTHER FACTORS TO CONSIDER**]—

As we've said, mentoring is called for whenever an employee seeks career-related advice. But what do you do if that employee is not yet great, that is, does not exceed expectations?

Use some combination of mentoring and coaching to address both long-term career aspirations and the employee's performance in the current job. The balance between the two depends on the extent of the employee's performance deficiencies. For example, you would spend more time on mentoring an employee like Productive Pat than you would one like Rockin' Robin (from Tool #10).

Also, it is possible that the optimal next step in an employee's career is outside of your organization. This could include going back to school full time to get an advanced degree or even employment elsewhere. We urge that you do not evade this or try to convince employees to stay against their best interests.

It is better to have a loyal and dedicated person on your team for a short time, who then leaves amicably, than a bitter and resentful person who quits in disgust and maligns you and your organization afterward.

APPLICATION

1. *Select* one employee you identified earlier in this tool who needs mentoring.

2. *Complete* the Mentoring Prep Sheet for that person.

3. *Review* and discuss your Prep Sheet with a *fellow manager* (whom you trust).

4. Review your Prep Sheet with *your* manager. Get advice and endorsement.

5. *Conduct* a mentoring meeting with the employee. (Refer to the Four Steps of a Coaching or Mentoring Dialogue in Tool #10.)

Turn On Teamwork

---[**WHY TEAMS DON'T WORK**]---

In fact, most so-called "teams" do not work for one of two reasons:

1. They're not supported or encouraged by the surrounding organization and are not recognized or rewarded for their efforts.
2. They're not really teams, but merely groups (at best) or pseudoteams (at worst).

Teams without access to necessary resources that are discouraged from investing time in team activities, or find their results and recommendations ignored, eventually flounder in frustration.

And if teams don't receive positive feedback for their efforts, teamwork won't be a positive value for them. To a great extent, people do what they are recognized for.

For the moment, though, let's assume that your organizational culture is conducive to teams and that management knows how to recognize them. We now focus on the second reason teams don't work: the attributes of the "team" itself.

GROUPS VS. TEAMS

What do we mean by the terms *group and team*? Generally, a group is three or more people who have something in common. Many such groups, for example, people stuck in traffic together, all retirees, or people who like vanilla ice cream...would never be mistaken for teams.

In the workplace, however, a working group often is mistaken for a team.

The following list describes the essential attributes, consequences, and examples of the various kinds of "teams" identified by Katzenbach and Smith in *The Wisdom of Teams* (also plotted on their *Team Performance Curve*, Figure 12-1):

- A *working group* is any number of people who work in the same setting and share, or profess to share, a common set of concerns. Much of what distinguishes a mere working group from a team relates to accountability. Working group members are individually accountable for specific goals, but there is no joint effort or mutual accountability.

  Their output is *the sum* of the individual contributions (not bad, but not all that they can be).

  Examples are common and include most organizations and departments. An example in sports is the U.S. Figure Skating Team, whose members train and compete as individuals or pairs.

- Much worse is a *pseudoteam*, which is a group of people, often a large group, who call themselves a team, although not functioning as such, and whose interactions actually detract from each member's individual performance.

  Their output is *much less* than the sum of the individual contributions.

  Examples often are notorious and include most committees, the U.S. Congress, and the 1994 U.S. Women's Figure Skating Team (Nancy Kerrigan and Tonya Harding).

- A *real team*, on the other hand, is a small number of people, ideally five to ten, who take the risks of *joint* action and work product. They have specific goals and a common approach for which they hold themselves individually and *mutually* accountable. Real team

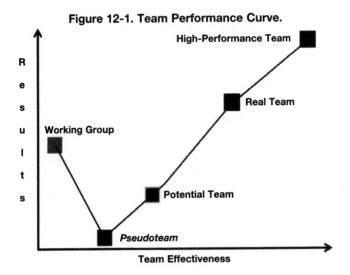

Figure 12-1. Team Performance Curve.

members also possess complementary skills—functional, problem solving, and interpersonal. They are committed to a meaningful purpose focused on performance.

Their output is *more* than the sum of individual contributions.

Examples are noteworthy and include orchestras, many sports teams, some quality teams, and the cast of the television show *Friends*.

- The ultimate in team effectiveness is the *high-performance team*. Such teams possess all the attributes of a real team, plus a deep commitment to each other's personal growth and success.

  Their output is *much more* than the sum of individual contributions.

  Examples are inspiring and include the 1980 U.S. Olympic Hockey Team, the heroes of 9/11, and the *Apollo 13* team.

- A *potential team* has begun the process of taking joint action, but it is still in an early stage of development. (In team development lingo, it is "forming" or "storming.") The risks the members are taking have not yet paid off.

  Their output (thus far) is *less* than the sum of the individual contributions.

  Examples are new teams and, perhaps, your team.

——————[**BRAINSTORMING AND CONSENSUS**]——————

Two of the interactive processes essential for the functioning of real teams are brainstorming and consensus.

Brainstorming is a freewheeling exchange of ideas without judgment or discussion, where team members build on each other's ideas. Done right, five to ten heads *are* better than one.

Beyond that basic statement, you really need to experience brainstorming to get it and your team needs to practice brainstorming—preferably with a seasoned facilitator—to actualize its potential. (We provide a few guidelines as part of the first application in this tool.)

Consensus also needs to be experienced and practiced, but an intellectual understanding of what it is (and isn't) is useful.

Consensus is the best thinking of all group members.

How do you obtain the best thinking? Let's first specify what you do not do. You do not vote! A unanimous vote (representing everyone's first priorities) is highly unlikely. A majority vote might not be supported by the minority.

Consensus is reaching a decision acceptable enough that no team member opposes it. This might not sound all that exciting, but it means that all members can support the decision.

Think about the significance of this proposition. If, indeed, the team members possess necessary complementary skills, then the opinions and buy-in of every member are critical to the team's success.

So if they don't vote, how does a team reach consensus? Often, they start with brainstorming to generate ideas and potential solutions. Then they zero in on, and tweak, the best ideas by using well-honed communication skills like listening and assertion (see Tools #8 and #16), tuning in to each other's nonverbal cues, and practicing RESPECT. (See the Introduction.)

APPLICATION #1

1. *Gather* your team together. (For this purpose, it does not matter what type of team they are.)

2. *Brainstorm* ideas for a team name and/or logo. (Just ideas; no decision yet.)

    • Give everyone a minute or two of silence to think about it.

    • Select a recorder who writes down **all** ideas on a flip chart.

    • Invite everyone to call out ideas—*no* holding back, discussion, or comments.

    • Encourage people to hitchhike—build upon ideas generated by others.

3. Take a *break*—a few minutes or a few days.

4. Meet again to *decide* on the team name and/or logo using consensus. (At least for the purpose of the activity. You don't have to publish the name/logo to others.)

5. During the next few days, *talk about* what the brainstorming and consensus experiences were like—in meetings and informally.

    • What went well? What could have gone better?

    • How do brainstorming and consensus compare with your team's normal ways of generating ideas and reaching decisions? List the pros and cons.

    • For what purposes might your team want to utilize either or both processes?

─┤ HIGH RISK/HIGH REWARD ├─

It is because of the dramatic results of real or high-performance teams that team-building training and activities are in such demand, and that this tool has been included in this book. But as we've shown, attempting to act as a team can be risky! And even if successful, the short-term results are minimal. (Notice the positions of pseudo and potential teams on the *Team Performance Curve*. See Figure 12-1.)

If you already have a reasonably effective working group, you may be better off not attempting it. Especially if:

1. You have doubts about your group's willingness to take risks and hold themselves mutually accountable

2.   There is insufficient organizational support

3.   Quick results are a priority

However, if the commitment and organizational support are there and you're willing and able to stick it out for the long haul, the results can be spectacular! And the sense of camaraderie and personal fulfillment experienced by team members is unrivaled.

By teaching essential team skills and processes, facilitating interpersonal bonding and trust, providing guidance through the inevitable stages of team development, and coaching how to handle common problems, an experienced team leader (or qualified trainer/facilitator) can help ensure that a potential team successfully transitions to a real team.

And if that extra personal commitment to each other exists, or can be ignited, they may even become a high-performance team.

MORE ON TEAMWORK AND TEAM BUILDING

Teamwork is a set of principles and skills unto itself. A more comprehensive treatment of this topic would include the stages of team development, common problems with teams (and what to do about them), team-building activities, and so on. To explore this subject further, see the Resource Guide.

APPLICATION #2

1.   *Think about* your work group in light of this tool.

2.   What *kind* of team is it?

3.   How *effective* is the team?

4.   If it is *not* a real or high-performance team, would you *like* it to be?

   • Is it *worth* the time and effort? (Do not kid yourself.)

   • What *barriers* exist? (Reflect on the High Risk/High Reward section.)

5.   *How* could the team become more effective, even without transformation to a real team?

5

Personal and Interpersonal Effectiveness

LIFE SKILLS

Part 3 dealt with communication skills especially relevant for leaders in influencing and guiding employees. In this part, we explore the more general (and fundamental) skill set necessary for personal and interpersonal effectiveness in the workplace…and in life.

Tool #13 unravels job burnout—its increasing prevalence, negative consequences, indicators (including a Burnout Inventory), causes, and four arenas of attack to blow it away. Included is an application to help you minimize burnout.

Tool #14 addresses the broader issue of stress and how to stay on top of it. You will discover what stress really is, the thinking processes at its root, and the personality traits that encourage a stress response.

In Tool #15, you'll learn about the importance of attitude—and how to improve it. We present three types of people exhibiting three different attitudes, describe what such attitudes look and sound like, demonstrate the importance of a positive attitude, and teach you how to transform your attitude by using self-talk and six other tips. Included are several activities to apply all of this to your own life.

Tool #16 unlocks assertion. Starting with a self-assessment, you'll learn what assertion really is—contrasted with aggression and submission, why it is a virtue, and how to become more assertive. Also included are a workplace scenario, suggested applications, and a 10-point guideline for dealing with difficult people.

Tool #17 unveils the five rules of anger: how to acknowledge it, experience it, process it, express it, and then let it go, effectively and nonviolently.

Tool #18 reveals the various manifestations and potentially devastating impact of change including how to deal with the fear that change often triggers, and describes six steps to rise to the challenge.

13

Blow Away Burnout

THE PLAGUE OF THE NEW MILLENNIUM

A 2005 study by the Families and Work Institute found that one-third of all U.S. employees are chronically overworked.

Many of us are working longer hours. But even more significant is the way we work today. Especially important is an increasing inability to focus on our work because of constant interruptions and distractions and excessive multitasking (required to keep up with all that has to be done).

Other factors identified in that study include:

- Job pressure: not enough time to get everything done
- Low-value work: spending time doing things perceived as a waste of time
- Accessibility: contact with work outside normal work hours
- Working while on vacation...or unused vacation

The consequences? The more overworked employees are, the more likely they are to make mistakes at work, feel angry at their employers, and resent their coworkers.

In addition to such work-related outcomes are personal ones: higher levels of stress, poorer health, self-neglect, and increased symptoms of clinical depression. In fact, the Families and Work Institute found that 26 percent of workers are often burned out or stressed by their work.

The St. Paul Fire and Marine Insurance Co. determined that problems at work are more strongly associated with health complaints than are any other life stressor; even more so than financial or family problems.

The monetary impact? It has been estimated that as much as $300 billion (or $7,500 per employee) is spent annually in the United States on stress-related:

- Compensation claims, health insurance costs, and direct medical expenses
- Absenteeism, employee turnover, and reduced productivity

Tool #2 addressed what employers can do to ameliorate the negative impact of job demands. This tool unlocks what individuals can do for themselves, that is, how you can alleviate your own job burnout and how your employees can alleviate theirs.

THE *SECRET* TO ALLEVIATING JOB BURNOUT

What do we mean by burnout? In general, it's feeling like our inner resources are inadequate to cope with situations. Burnout is a form of excessive stress or our reaction to ongoing stress. Job burnout is feeling this way about work, where the situations are job related.

The *Secret* (or, at least, the first step) to blowing it away is:

Acknowledge how burned-out you are.

We suggest you take a minute or two to complete the following Burnout Inventory Worksheet.

Worksheet 13-1. Am I Burned-Out...or What!?

For each of the following statements, rate to what extent the symptom has been true for you recently (especially at work) using this scale:

Rarely/Not Really 1 — 2 — 3 — 4 — 5 Usually/Definitely

Please be candid. This is *for your eyes only*!

___ 1. I get tired easily.

___ 2. I am dissatisfied with my work.

___ 3. I feel sad and don't know why.

___ 4. I've been forgetting things.

___ 5. I get grumpy and short-tempered.

___ 6. I have trouble sleeping due to worrying about work.

___ 7. I have more frequent illnesses.

___ 8. I don't have the same enthusiasm for my job.

___ 9. I've been getting into conflicts with others.

___ 10. My job performance has dropped.

___ 11. I use alcohol or drugs to feel better.

___ 12. Communicating with others is a strain.

___ 13. I've been having difficulty concentrating.

___ 14. I am easily bored with work.

___ 15. I work hard, but feel like I accomplish little.

___ 16. I feel frustrated with my work.

___ 17. I don't like going to work.

___ 18. I spend less time with friends and family.

___ 19. I don't have much to look forward to in my work.

___ 20. I worry about work during my leisure time.

_____ = Total ← Now **add up** your ratings.

Adapted from *Overcoming Job Burnout: How to Renew Enthusiasm for Work*, by permission. Copyright 1980, 1993, 1998, and 2005: Beverly A. Potter. www.docpotter.com.

How did you do? If you scored 20–40, you are **Cool** and probably do not need to read the rest of this tool, unless you suspect that some of your employees would not do as well. (**Note:** If you scored less than 20, you either cheated or should take a second look at the instructions.)

More likely, however, is that you are **Gettin' Warm** (40–60). If so, you are fortunate, because you're catching the problem at an early stage and can address it before it gets worse. This tool's **Cool Tips** can help.

Or, maybe you are **Starting to Burn** (60–80). This is a bit more serious. Burnout probably is impacting your health and your performance. Our **Cool Tips** are highly recommended.

If you scored 80–100, you're **Toast!** In which case you should immediately and aggressively begin applying our **Cool Tips** and, perhaps, seek personalized assistance from a medical/mental health professional.

Another way to assess burnout level, in yourself or in your employees, is to look for any of the signs of job burnout:

The Signs of Job Burnout

1. Chronic fatigue: exhausted, rundown, and so on
2. Negative, irritable, critical of self, easily angered
3. Feeling overwhelmed
4. Frequent headaches or gastrointestinal upset
5. Weight loss or gain
6. Shortness of breath
7. Feelings of helplessness
8. Anxiety/panic attacks, depression
9. Declining productivity
10. Interpersonal problems

Also check to see whether any of these job-related causes of burnout are applicable to you or your employees:

Causes of Job Burnout

1. Feeling unable to meet job expectations
2. Feeling your true abilities are underutilized

3. Poor relationship with supervisor
4. Difficult relationships with coworkers or customers
5. Unappreciated for good work
6. Lack of timely feedback or praise from supervisor
7. Feeling supervisor does not listen to your issues
8. Feeling left out of things
9. Changes in business or work environment
10. Inability to balance personal and professional life

Once you acknowledge that you are burned-out (to whatever extent), what can you do about it? There are four arenas of attack: physical, mental, interpersonal, and spiritual—our four **Cool Tips.**

Cool Tip #1:
The Physical Arena

This tip is pretty straightforward:

1. Get a physical exam: How is burnout impacting your health?
2. Eat healthy: all four food groups in moderation...no fad diets or bingeing.
3. Exercise: regularly, moderately, appropriate to your age and condition.
4. Practice relaxation...

In our workshops, we teach four different relaxation techniques. Here's one of them:

THE PURIFYING BREATH

1. Begin by closing your eyes and just become aware of your breathing without any attempt to modify it. Focus only on your breathing. Tune out any distractions or concerns. Notice how

your belly rises as you breathe in and subsides as you breathe out. Just relax and focus on your breathing. Do this for as long as you like.

2.   When ready, take a deep breath by inhaling slowly through your nose deeply into your abdomen and completely filling your lungs.

3.   Hold this breath for as long as you comfortably can.

4.   When ready, exhale even more slowly through your mouth, pushing all the air out.

5.   Repeat Steps 2–4 several times.

6.   Open your eyes.

How do you feel?

(For more information on relaxation, see The Art of Relaxation at the end of this tool and the Resource Guide.)

Cool Tip #2:
The Mental Arena

Ultimately, stress is internally generated; it is how you process external triggers of burnout.

1.   Develop or improve coping skills. (See the rest of Part 5.) These coping skills are perhaps best summarized by the Serenity Prayer, which can be viewed either as a religious prayer or a secular self-dedication:

...grant me the **Serenity** to accept the things I cannot change
Courage to change the things I can
and the **Wisdom** to know the difference.

2.   Understand your strengths and weaknesses. Capitalize on your strengths and find ways to shore up your weaknesses, for example, through others and/or self-improvement.

3. Learn effective (not so much time management) but inner resource management:

   - Take breaks
   - Relax during your time off (and work breaks)
   - Delegate and/or swap tasks with others
   - Ask for time off and use all allotted vacation time

4. Set realistic goals: goals that are important to *you*, not to please others, and that are challenging but attainable.

5. Learn to schedule "me time": not for work, family, or friends, but for *you*.

6. Consult your Employee Assistance Program (EAP), a life-skills coach, or mental health counselor. You consult professionals for your financial or legal affairs, why not for your mental well-being?

Cool Tip #3:
The Interpersonal Arena

Are your relationships with others enhancing the quality of your life or diminishing it?

1. Nurture close relationships: Spend quality time with your loved ones.

2. Participate in clubs, associations, and group activities that relax and enrich you; eliminate those that do not.

3. Address ongoing issues with supervisor, coworkers, family, and friends. Listen to their needs and assert yourself. (See Tools #8 and #16.)

4. Consider a job/career/life change. However, avoid making changes out of anger, desperation, or panic. Instead, seek other options and wait until you are ready to make a logical, rational decision.

Cool Tip #4:
The Spiritual Arena

By spiritual, we don't mean anything weird or mystical. Rather, we mean a cleansing of the soul or nurturing your inner self. It includes:

1. Religion: whatever that may be for you, especially prayer and confession, or their secular counterparts:

   Meditation: a very deep and focused form of relaxation

   Psychotherapy and support groups: where you share your deepest secrets

2. The Arts: performing or experiencing music, dance, theatre, graphic arts, and so on

3. Hobbies: those that engage your attention and leave you feeling relaxed and fulfilled

4. Volunteer work: contributing your time to a cause you find meaningful

---

APPLICATION

1. Think about *your lifestyle* in light of the four arenas and the specific suggestions included in each.

2. Are there arenas of your life that you've been *shortchanging?*
   For example:

   Are you a couch potato? Focus especially on the physical arena.

   Are you a very other-focused person? Concentrate on mental and spiritual arenas.

   Do you keep mostly to yourself? Focus especially on the interpersonal arena.

3. Are there *specific aspects* of any arena that ring true for you?
   For example:

   Are you a very social person? Perhaps you need to nurture close relationships more.

   Are you a workaholic? Perhaps you need to manage your inner resources more.

Do you work hard and play hard? Perhaps you need to slow down a bit and relax.

4. Start making *changes* in your life—gradually, one step at a time. Move especially toward those activities that appeal to you, even if you have to get past some initial resistance. For example:

    If you used to play in a band, don't force yourself to take up stamp collecting. Instead, get back into music.

    If, as a child you loved swimming, get back into the water.

    If you have a solid relationship with your spouse but no longer feel in love, take a romantic second honeymoon.

    If you used to love reading adventure novels, budget time to do so again.

The Art of Relaxation

Relaxation is the foundation of any stress or burnout reduction program. It induces a state of being, where you can feel actual physical and psychological changes.

Major benefits include:

1. Decreases in the body's heightened tension.
2. Allows a more rational response to stressors.
3. Increases awareness and makes the mind clearer.
4. Helps to recover more quickly from illness, pain, and trauma.

Guidelines for practicing relaxation

1. Find a quiet environment
2. Get comfortable
3. Do not worry about your performance
4. Accept yourself
5. Stay focused
6. Set aside a regular time just for relaxation

Relaxation aids

1. Soothing music or nature sounds
2. Visualize/remember peaceful scenes
3. Massage or gentle touching
4. Yoga
5. A warm bath or hot tub
6. Whatever comforts you

Stay on Top of Stress

In the previous tool, we defined burnout as a form of excessive stress or our reaction to ongoing stress. This tool unlocks stress itself.

The 1997 National Study of the Changing Workforce found that 36 percent of employees often feel drained or used up at the end of a workday. Even more troubling, employees reported feeling tired *before* the workday begins.

Was this just a twentieth-century phenomenon? Let's take a look:

- In 1998, *Human Resource News* reported that "stress has increased dramatically as a reason why today's employees are missing work, almost tripling since 1995."

- Four years later, *Fortune* magazine (October 2002) reported that "stress in the workplace is skyrocketing and has reached record levels."

- In 2005, a Families and Work study found that "26 percent of workers are often very burned out or stressed by their work."

No, stress is not going away. And there are long-term implications of stress. Anyone experiencing ongoing stress provides a fertile breeding ground for illness. These illnesses range from the common cold to more severe problems, such as heart attacks and strokes.

—[## WHAT IS STRESS?]—

Simply put, stress is any strain on the body or mind. In a sense, there are two types:

1. External: those life events and outside stressors like job demands or personal losses that trigger a stress response.

2. Internal: how we process those external triggers.

The bottom line is that stress is a *choice*.

-   You can eliminate the external stressor. For example, if your boss is getting you down, you can quit your job. Often, however, that is not an option.

-   Perhaps you can modify the external situation, for example, try to influence your boss to change his or her ways.

-   And you always have a third option—choose to be less affected by it: "The serenity to accept the things I cannot change."

—[## UNDERSTANDING THE FUNDAMENTALS OF STRESS]—

What causes stress? An overdemanding job? The juggling of work and family responsibilities? Having to deal with other stressed people?

Well, believe it or not, stress is what we do to ourselves. All those external event stressors that seem like stress really are just triggers of our own erroneous thoughts. Stop and think for a moment about any events that you've found stressful. What thoughts were going through your mind during those events? We suspect that those thoughts have been self-conflicting. And probably some variation on "I must and I can't!"

Let's say a member of your staff does something that you regard as intolerable, for example, misses a deadline, mistreats a customer, or violates a safety procedure. Now, none of these behaviors should be ignored; you should feel compelled to take appropriate action. But, in addition, you'll probably experience stress.

Here's the two-edged reason why:

1.   The very fact that you regard the behavior as intolerable; not just undesirable, but unacceptable, that is, you believe you *can't* accept it.

2.   You recognize that you *must* accept it.

In other words, "I can't" is at war with "I must." In this case, *must* is closer to the truth than *can't*. The behavior occurred, like it or not, and you bear the consequences for it. You have a responsibility—not for the employee's behavior itself—but to take corrective action.

Note the clarification. Believing that you are directly responsible for the behavior of others is a common, but erroneous, source of stress. It's especially prevalent among parents, of course, but managers also often fall victim. More on this follows.

To compound the tension, you tell yourself that you *must* take corrective action, but you don't know what to do, that is, you *can't*. Perhaps you've had insufficient training or experience to handle such matters effectively…or your authority or freedom of action is restricted in some way…or the employee has been unreceptive to coaching in the past…or a combination of these. You believe that you *can't* correct the situation.

It is the internal conflict between absolutes, such as "I must" and "I can't," that is the root of all stress. It is the classic irresistible force and immovable object. Your very being knows that the conflict, as stated, cannot be resolved and you feel a rush of anxiety, worry, and/or guilt.

So how do you resolve it? By challenging either or both of those (erroneous) absolutes. Reframe the *must* to *want* and the *can't* to *can*. Sound simplistic? Well sometimes it is simple, but not necessarily easy.

In the aforementioned example, *can* may involve effort, for example, study, thought, or asking for assistance, advice, or authority to act. In general, this reframing requires extensive practice to become a habit, as well as a rethinking of many of your most closely held precepts, or fundamental convictions. Such flawed logic usually is deeply rooted and reinforced by the world around you.

For example, we expect that you might take issue with our assertion that you are not responsible for the actions of others. Do we seem to be challenging a key principle of leadership (or parenthood)? Actually, we are challenging what we hold to be a misstatement of that principle. We maintain that leaders influence, rather than control and deal with the consequences of their employees' actions, rather than being the direct cause of the actions.

Another example of faulty thinking is the belief—widely held, especially among men—that asking for help is a sign of weakness: "I can't appear weak." Actually, asking for help is a sign of maturity and self-esteem.

And sometimes the rethinking required may not be simple. For example, the source of erroneous conflict can be contained in multiple meanings of the same word. Take the word *responsible*. *The American Heritage Dictionary* defines it as "involving personal accountability" and "being a source or cause."

If you are a leader, you are accountable for your organization's performance: "The buck stops here." But as stated previously, although you are expected to influence others, you are not the direct source or cause of the actions of individual employees. You cannot control other people. To attempt to do so produces stress and makes other people miserable. Any of us who has ever worked for a micromanager knows that secondary consequence all too well.

Philosopher/novelist Ayn Rand called such multiple-meaning words *conceptual package deals*—using one word to package, simultaneously, two different, conflicting concepts. We are not referring to different words that are spelled the same. For example, *lie* can mean either "recline" or "falsehood," but never both at the same time (other than as a deliberate play on words). In a conceptual package deal, however, you hold in your mind both meanings at the same time.

Another way to think of package concepts is as a special type of connotation, that is, the value-laden flavor that words can have. For example, *abrupt* literally means "unexpectedly sudden." When describing a person's behavior, it has the connotation of curt, rude, or brusque.

Unlike many connotations, however, the connotations of package concepts are multiple and conflicting. *Abrupt* does not connote both rude and polite. But for many of us, *responsible* connotes both: "It's appropriate for me to handle the consequences of that action" and "I caused that action in the first place." The latter is valid only if we are talking about one's own behavior. To make matters worse, because of their crippling effects, responsible often packages negative concepts like fault and blame as well.

Even the word *must* can be a package concept. Often, we misuse it to mean "it is important that" or "strongly desire to" while also holding in our minds the absolute compulsion (and dire consequences) involved with "have to" or "no choice." *Can't* also is often misused to mean "have difficulty" or "be uncertain," but without giving up the paralyzing effect of "unable."

Here's a sampling of some other workplace-related stress-inducing package concepts:

- **Loyalty:** "full commitment to the stated values of the employer" (or perhaps, "never betraying the employment contract") ... packaged with "My company (or boss), right or wrong."
- **Policy:** "guideline for handling similar situations"...packaged with "absolute law."
- **Authority:** "The organization publicly supports my acting on my own judgment within this scope"...packaged with "My word is law" or "I have just enough rope to hang myself."
- **Employee:** "fellow human being with whom there is a contractual working relationship"...packaged with "property/servant/ child/subordinate/headcount."
- **Boss:** "responsible for providing direction, receiving reports, and evaluating performance"...packaged with "bully/master/father."
- **ASAP:** "as soon as you can fit it into your other priorities"... packaged with "Hop to it!"

We are sure you can think of many more examples.

In the next tool, you'll learn a powerful technique to overcome such stress-inducing package concepts—transforming your self-talk.

─┤ VULNERABLE PERSONALITY TRAITS ├─

Some personality traits encourage a stress response. Notice if you recognize yourself (or your employees) in any of the following:

- Perfectionist
- Overreactive

- Sensitive to criticism
- Obsessive
- Worrier
- Suggestible to the problems of others
- Extremely high expectations (of self and others)
- Need to appear in control
- Guilt-ridden: "shoulda; coulda; woulda"

If you see some of these traits in yourself, perhaps you need an attitude adjustment—the subject of our next tool.

Accentuate the Positive

Tool #14 ended with the proposition that effective stress management entails adjusting one's attitude. But the significance of attitude extends far beyond stress.

Much of this book deals with optimizing individual performance. *The fundamental factor underlying the successful application of all other performance factors is attitude.* Unfortunately, too often attitude is dismissed as something we are cursed (or blessed) with and unable to change or is just too intangible to deal with objectively in the workplace.

All of these attitudes about attitude are incorrect and counterproductive. A person's attitude, both fundamental view of life and specific views of various life challenges, is reflected in objective behavior and can be changed—not manipulated by outside forces, but transformed by the individual.

This tool examines the nature of attitude, why it's important, three different attitudes (and how they are reflected in behavior), and how to transform attitude with self-talk. Also included is an activity to gauge your own attitude and six additional tips for improving it.

WHAT IS ATTITUDE?

Attitude is the underlying way we think, feel, and act: how we react to the world around us. It determines the quality and effectiveness of all of our thinking, emotions, and behavior and, thereby, the positive or negative consequences of that behavior.

Attitude is the one thing we can count on as a lifetime companion. Jobs and relationships come and go, but your attitude is always with you. You can't take a vacation from yourself!

Attitude is based upon our expectations and perceptions—our definition of reality.

THREE TYPES OF PEOPLE, THREE DIFFERENT ATTITUDES

Each of the following individuals has the same job, but notice the different attitudes:

Susan Spectator likes the predictability and limited responsibility of her job. She feels most comfortable when others make the important decisions. Susan feels threatened when anything out of the norm happens and immediately calls her manager for instructions. She never feels certain about anything and has difficulty making commitments.

Carl Critic feels frustrated in his job, but it at least gives him a chance to complain and vent his frustrations about all the "idiots" he deals with. When confronted with his mistakes, he looks for excuses and others to blame. Carl hates what he regards as impositions placed on him by coworkers and customers. His negative opinions are known by all.

Paula Player views her job as an opportunity to experience the thrill of competence and meeting progressive challenges. She enjoys interacting with her coworkers, customers, and management. When Paula makes a mistake, she acknowledges it to herself and to those impacted by it and then looks to see how she can correct and learn from it.

Susan Spectator, Carl Critic, and Paula Player exemplify three very different ways of approaching life and relating to others—three very different attitudes:

1. **Spectators with Neutral Attitudes:** Spectators watch life happen and observe others. They play it safe and try to avoid risks. Spectators are afraid of change. They often are tired or detached. Their defining word is "Maybe." Their prevailing action is "Coast." Their typical phrases are "I doubt it, I might, I don't know," and "I'm hesitant."

2. **Critics with Negative Attitudes:** Critics comment on life and complain. They critique after the fact, imposing their "expertise" and finding fault in others. Critics are annoyed by change. They often appear frustrated or pessimistic. Their defining word is "No!" Their prevailing action is "Stop!" Their typical phrases are "I can't, I won't, No way," and "You made me."

3. **Players with Positive Attitudes:** Players actively participate in life and embrace opportunities. They take risks and are willing to make mistakes. Players enjoy learning and change. They usually are confident and optimistic. Their defining word is "Yes!" Their prevailing action is "Go!" Their typical phrases are "I can, I will, I'm sure," and "I choose to."

Adapted from *Attitude: The Choice Is Yours,* by Michele Matt, CSP, Book Marketing Solutions, 2007.

Most of us embody some of each type of person and attitude. Often, though, one general attitude predominates.

WHAT ATTITUDES LOOK LIKE

As you see, attitudes are communicated by what you say (or do not say) and how you say it. They also are communicated by what you look like (your facial expressions and body language). For example:

Neutral	Negative	Positive
Expressionless	Frown	Smile
Cry	Groan	Laugh
Daydream	Quarrel	Act, enthusiastically
Arms at sides	Arms crossed	Open arms in motion
Folded hands	Fists/Pointed fingers	Open hands in motion
Eyes averted	Piercing eyes	Eye contact
Jaw slack	Jaw jutted forward	Jaw relaxed

WHY IS ATTITUDE IMPORTANT?

A study of success factors by Telemetrics International surveyed 16,000 people. The study found that one of the most significant differences between high and low achievers was their attitude!

Let's look at two examples from figure skating:

1. Sarah Hughes won the Olympic Gold Medal in 2002. She had far less experience and probably less raw talent than her main competition, Michelle Kwan and Irena Slutskaya, whom she trailed as they entered the final stage of the competition, the free skate. Sarah won the free skate and the championship by skating her heart out—"the performance of a lifetime." She was in the moment.

    While her competitors were plagued by the pressure of expectations and, therefore, by mistakes, Sarah skated flawlessly and with pure joy. Also of note is her close relationship with her very supportive coach, Robin Wagner. (See Tip #4 of this tool.)

2. Tonya Harding, on the other hand, performed dismally in an earlier Olympic competition. A two-time national champion, Tonya was the first American woman to complete a triple Axel in major

competition. She certainly had the talent. Tonya Harding is remembered, however, as being implicated in the brutal attack on her teammate, Nancy Kerrigan (who went on to win the Olympic Silver Medal).

Tonya, a high school dropout and now twice divorced, often blamed outside factors (e.g., her skate laces) for mistakes in her performance. At that time, she was married to a truly sleazy man, who, for example, arranged the attack on Kerrigan. In interviews and photos, Tonya often appeared sad and insecure, even while smiling.

GOOD NEWS AND BAD NEWS

The bad news: We cannot control everything that happens to us. (Isn't that a bummer?) Nancy Kerrigan certainly did not plan on being bashed in the knee shortly before the Olympics. Sarah Hughes could not count on mistakes being made by her competitors.

The good news: The one thing we can always control is our attitude! Even before learning that she had won the Gold Medal (due, in part, to luck), Sarah Hughes knew that she had done her personal best. Nancy Kerrigan wasn't quite as lucky—she won "only" Silver. But Nancy also knew that she had turned in a transcendent performance, despite her injury.

You do control your attitude:

No one can make you feel anything
without your permission!

When we make this statement in our training classes, participants often take issue with it. Perhaps you do as well.

We are not referring to children or to victims of physical violence, nor to the transitory emotions triggered by external events, rather, to an adult's basic state of emotional well-being and self-esteem.

For example, the attack on Nancy Kerrigan was captured on video.

She certainly experienced pain and anguish at that time. But it didn't affect her attitude or her Olympic performance. (Fortunately, the physical damage to her knee was not incapacitating.)

And here's the payoff:

Control of your attitude ⟶ Control of your life!

APPLICATION #1

1. *Recall* a challenge you faced in your interactions with others (whether in your current job, in a previous job, or in your personal life).

2. *Describe* the situation, the other people involved, what was challenging about it, and how you handled it.

    > What were your actions? Your thoughts? Your feelings?

    > What statements did you use? In what tone of voice?

    > What was your body language? Your facial expression?

3. Now *step back* and look at what you've written. Were you a *Spectator, Critic,* or *Player* (or some combination)?

4. How could you face and handle a similar challenge in the *future?*

⎾ SELF-TALK ⏌

More good news: A negative or neutral attitude can always be changed! One way to do this, perhaps the most powerful, is by listening to your self-talk and changing negative statements to positive ones.

We communicate every moment of our lives, not only with others but also with ourselves. Much of this self-talk comes from a tape in our mind.

Most of the data on that tape was recorded during early learning experiences; some came later.

By the time we are 17 years old, we have taken in and recorded 150,000 pieces of negative data! For example: "You can't...You shouldn't ...You'll only fail ...Don't try...Who are you to ...?"

Garbage In ➞ Garbage Out

This computer programming expression is applicable to mental programming as well. If you fill your mind with negative thoughts, you will have a negative attitude. And this negative attitude will poison your actions, resulting in negative consequences.

Fortunately, all these negative thoughts can be *transformed* into positive thoughts, attitudes, and actions...and consequences!

Monitor your self-talk. Catch yourself using negative words and phrases and replace them with positive dialogue.

For example:

- ~~I am a failure~~ ➞ I have not yet succeeded.
- ~~I messed up~~ ➞ That did not turn out the way I wanted. I will try again.
- ~~I am a mistake~~ ➞ That was a mistake. Okay. What can I learn from it?

APPLICATION #2

1. Write down some of *your negative thoughts* and/or negative statements you have made about yourself, your job, or others.

2. *Think about* what you've written. How accurate or fair are these thoughts or statements?

3. Try *reframing* each thought into a more accurate, fair, and *positive* statement.

—⌈   # HOW TO CHANGE YOUR
SELF-TALK   ⌉—

There are four steps and each is important:

1. ***Recognize:*** Start paying attention to your internal dialogue, especially when feeling disappointed or frustrated. What are you saying to yourself? It's probably negative and untrue or unfair. Very likely, it's unduly harsh.

    And don't limit this to major issues. Our sense of ourselves is formed primarily by our thoughts about the little things, the typos of life. If you do this often enough regarding your minute-by-minute thoughts and actions, you will be well prepared to face the big challenges.

2. ***STOP!*** Tell yourself: "STOP!"...or words/images to that effect. For example, Sheryl often visualizes a blinking red stoplight. Don usually says "No! That's not true!"

    You do not deserve the kind of negative judgments you may have been making about yourself.

3. ***Restate:*** But don't leave it at that. It's very important to reframe the negative statement into a positive and more accurate one. For example, change "I'll never be able to do this!" to "That was a bit disappointing. Oh well, better next time."

    For extra credit, and to become more effective in action, you may add, "Let's see, what can I learn from this? How can I do it better next time?"

4. ***Reward:*** If you have the time and money, you can take yourself on a shopping spree. More often, however, we suggest that you pat yourself on the back. (And don't hesitate to do this literally, particularly in private.) For example, "Hey! I did it! Well done!"

Those are the four steps to take every time you notice a negative thought. But, in a sense, there's a fifth step, as well: ***Practice!***

Reframing just one or two negative thoughts isn't going to help that much. Remember, you are challenging a lifetime of negative programming. As with any other skill, you need to keep practicing this four-step process until this transformation becomes a habit.

SIX ADDITIONAL TIPS FOR A MORE POSITIVE ATTITUDE

Tip 1: Stay in the present tense.

You cannot change the past. And you cannot yet take action in the future. What you've been given to work with is the present.

In which of these do you spend most of your mental life? Ruminating about the past? Worrying about the future? (By the way, although planning is effective, worrying is totally unproductive, even counterproductive.)

Or are you in the moment; fully focused on what you're thinking, feeling, and doing at this time? Be...Here...Now!

THE CIRCLE OF IMAGINATION

Before reading Tip #2 we recommend that you try this brief two-part visualization exercise:

1.   Imagine that you're part of a circle of people. Place in the center of the circle a loved one, for example, a child, spouse, or friend. Imagine that your loved one is in anguish, feeling pain and fear and, perhaps, crying. What do you feel impelled to do or say to that person?

Do not go on to the second part of this exercise
until you complete this visualization.

2. You are still part of that circle. But this time, put yourself in the center of the circle. That's right, simultaneously, you are in the center *and* you are watching yourself from the rim. Imagine that the "you" in the center is in anguish, feeling pain and fear and, perhaps, crying. What do you (the observer) feel impelled to do or say to that person?

Now reflect on what you said or did in the two visualizations. Any differences? Most people are more compassionate, supportive, and nurturing with the loved one than with themselves. That's a shame. Don't you deserve the same level of compassion as you give your loved ones?

Tip 2: Talk to yourself in a calming, compassionate manner.

If you entered the Circle of Imagination, you may have discovered that you tend not to do this. But we hope you agree that you deserve such treatment.

For example, replace "Get your act together, [your last name]!" with "It's okay, [your nickname], just relaaaxxx."

And please address yourself fondly, for example, use your nickname, rather than your last name (as a drill sergeant, stuffy teacher, or cold boss might).

Tip 3: Talk yourself out of unreasonable expectations and fearful thoughts.

Use the same technique as you did for self-talk. Really challenge those expectations and fears. How reasonable, realistic, or likely are the events you are projecting? If they're not reasonable, tell yourself to "Stop!"...and reframe your expectations to more likely (and less alarming) ones.

If you really do think your expectations are reasonable (but undesirable), try to come to terms with them. Even people facing certain death sometimes are able to become accepting and serene.

Tip 4: Surround yourself with positive people.

It is difficult, although not impossible, to remain positive while those around you are naysayers and critics. Compare Sarah Hughes's coach and family with Tonya Harding's husband and dismal childhood.

Definitely separate yourself from the optional relationships in your life (e.g., significant others, friends, acquaintances) that are sucking your energy, self-confidence, and self-worth. Start reaching out to those who give you what you need—the positive strokes and shared values.

You may even want to consider separating from employment and familial relationships that are not fulfilling. If that is not feasible, or if it is a mixed bag, begin asserting yourself and modifying the implicit ground rules of the relationship. (See Tool #16.)

Tip 5: Do not "should" on yourself.

Shoulds are expectations that we usually fall short of because they tend to be what matters more to other people—perhaps people from the past, like our parents, whose dictums we've internalized. This can lead to enormous stress on all parties concerned.

A *should* that you want to do is a *want*. Do it because you want to do it.

Take a second look at any *should* you don't want to do. Discover whether you really do want to (perhaps considering a broader context)...or eliminate it.

Test this technique with the *shoulds* that you use. For example, *should* you go to the dentist for a root canal? Perhaps the experience itself is unpleasant. But visualize the consequences of not doing it. If you really get in touch with the long-term benefit of the procedure, you probably will *want* to keep that dental appointment.

This is not just semantics. Such words have emotional impact. A *should* acts as a whip; you drag yourself to fulfill it. A want, on the other hand, is motivating and energizing. (See Tool #1.)

Tip 6: Take action!

This and Tool #14 are examples of the cognitive–behavioral approach to mental well-being. Most of the foregoing has focused on the cognitive aspect. Equally important is the behavioral. Just *doing* positive things (e.g., the Four Arenas of Attack in Tool #13) will improve your attitude.

Assert Yourself ... and Deal with "Difficult" People

In Tool #7, we compared and contrasted feedback with assertion, which we heartily advocated. And we've alluded to the importance of asserting yourself in the context of teamwork, job burnout, and attitude. (We will do so again in Tool #19 on harassment.) Tool #16 reveals assertiveness in greater depth.

We start with an opportunity to assess your current level of assertiveness. We describe what it is, contrast assertion with aggression (with which it is most often confused) and submission, enumerate why it is a virtue, illustrate assertion in a workplace scenario, offer guidelines on how to be assertive, and, of course, suggest an application.

This tool concludes with a 10-point guideline for dealing with difficult people by bringing together principles and skills from this and several preceding tools.

HOW ASSERTIVE ARE YOU?

We suggest you take a minute or two to complete the Assertion Self-Assessment. We urge you to be candid. It's for your eyes only.

Worksheet 16-1. Assertion Self-Assessment.

Indicate with a check mark the degree of comfort/discomfort you would feel in each of the following situations:

	Comfortable	Some Discomfort	NO Comfort
1. Confront a fellow coworker about a problem.	_____	_____	_____
2. Ask a friend for money he or she owes you.	_____	_____	_____
3. Apologize when you are at fault.	_____	_____	_____
4. Turn down a relative's request for a favor.	_____	_____	_____
5. Tell a friend he or she did something that offended you.	_____	_____	_____
6. Accept a compliment.	_____	_____	_____
7. State your opinion when it differs from an authority's.	_____	_____	_____
8. Request the return of something a friend borrowed.	_____	_____	_____
9. Tell coworkers when they treat you unfairly.	_____	_____	_____
10. Ask your partner for attention and affection.	_____	_____	_____
11. Look people in the eye when confronting them.	_____	_____	_____
12. Discuss with someone his or her criticism of you.	_____	_____	_____
13. Admit your fears.	_____	_____	_____
14. Tell others about your accomplishments.	_____	_____	_____
15. Ask someone to put out his or her cigarette.	_____	_____	_____

Adapted from *Attacking Anxiety*, Midwest Center for Stress and Anxiety, 1989.

Now step back and look at the pattern of your check marks. Are most of them in the Comfortable column? If so, and you were candid, you already are very assertive. To become even better at it, think about the items you checked in the other two columns and consciously work to be more assertive in the situation described, thereby becoming more comfortable.

Were most of your check marks in the Some Discomfort and NO Comfort columns? If so, there is definite room for improvement. You cannot really describe yourself as being assertive.

Notice the situations in which you are least comfortable:

- Are you less assertive in your worklife (situations 1, 7, and 9) than in your personal life (2, 4, 5, 8, and 10)...or vice versa?
- Are you especially uncomfortable in situations exposing emotional vulnerability (3, 10, and 13)?
- Are you less comfortable in situations affirming your self-worth (6, 7, and 14)?

Think especially about these areas of your life as you read this tool.

ASSERTION: WHAT IS IT?

Visualize Rosa Parks. Her simple but courageous act of quietly refusing to move from her seat at the front of the bus changed the world. That act embodies the true nature—and power—of assertion.

We've seen several definitions of assertion. This one is our favorite:

Assertion is speaking honestly about your thoughts, feelings, and desires, while considering those of others.

This is what I think/feel/want...and (at least implicitly)...how about you?

Sounds pretty good to us! Honesty. Respecting yourself and others. Considering its inherent uncontroversial virtues, it is puzzling that more people are not assertive.

Here's another, although more a description than a definition:

Assertion takes responsibility for solving interpersonal problems through straightforward action and communication.

When you assert, you take responsibility, you solve problems, and you are straightforward, rather than underhanded or devious.

The following definition is perhaps the most common, but our least favorite:

Assertion is a way of acting that strikes a balance between two extremes: aggression and submission.

This one is not entirely accurate. Instead of being a balance, assertion really is an alternative to the two sides of the same coin: aggression and submission.

In fact, aggression or submission is a consequence of *not* being assertive.

—⌐ **ALTERNATIVES TO ASSERTION** ⌐—

Aggression

- Is communicating in a demanding, abrasive, or hostile way
- Is insensitivity to the rights, thoughts, feelings, or desires of others
- Attempts to obtain results or responses through intimidation
- Creates a dominate–lose scenario that can lead to resentment and violence

Submission (or passivity)

- Is yielding to others' wants, while discounting your own rights
- Is an inability to express your thoughts, feelings, or desires
- Is feeling guilty when expressing desires, as if you are imposing
- Tears down self-esteem and confidence (and causes you to build up anger)

If you read the previous tool on attitude, you may see a parallel between negative/neutral/positive attitude and aggressive/submissive/assertive behavior. They are related.

Here's a quick way to identify true assertion (in yourself or others) versus submission or aggression:

Assertion says	Aggression adds	Submission says
This is what I think.	**Your** thoughts are absurd.	What I think isn't important.
This is what I feel.	**Your** feelings don't count.	What I feel doesn't matter.
This is what I want.	**Your** wants aren't important.	What I want doesn't count.

When people are not assertive, they gravitate to either aggression or submission, depending on personality type or mood. Often, the same individual will vacillate between aggression and submission, or act in ways that combine the two:

- *Passive–Aggressive:* expressing anger in a covert fashion, for example, "forgetting" about others' requests or plotting revenge.

- *Manipulative:* playing the victim or martyr to get others to feel sympathy for or take care of the manipulator.

THE VIRTUE OF ASSERTIVENESS

Assertion allows us to:

- Express ourselves honestly
- Consider how others feel
- Feel good about ourselves
- Take responsibility
- Negotiate productively
- Go for a win–win resolution

These are all obvious virtues and positive values! So why aren't many of us assertive more often? Well, the most prevalent reason is fear of rejection or disapproval. This is not an irrational fear. In fact, some people may not like what we are asserting. That is, they may not like us, at least that aspect of us, at that time. Being at peace with that disapproval requires healthy self-esteem. A discussion of the requirements of self-esteem is outside the scope of this book. (See the Resource Guide.) One thing we can say about it here is that an essential ingredient to building one's self-esteem is assertion. The more often we express ourselves honestly, the more we will feel good about ourselves.

A word of warning: Assertion is not a guarantee that you will get the response or results you want. There is no such guarantee. But, in addition to all the benefits enumerated, assertion stands a far better chance of getting those results than aggression or submission, at least in the long run and without the negative backlash inherent in those alternatives.

But should one *always* be assertive? We maintain that you should* always be assertive...in your thoughts, but not necessarily in voicing those thoughts. There very well may be circumstances in which the consequences of vocal assertion could be quite negative, for example, when dealing with an aggressive person in authority or when threatened with violence. (See Tool #21.)

Sometimes, maintaining silence is the wisest and most assertive action to take—not endorsement of another's actions or statements, but silence, or, perhaps, acknowledgement. Something like "I hear what you're saying," without adding "I agree."

ASSERTION SCENARIO

You have created a new, streamlined procedure that you showed to one of your coworkers, prior to showing it to your boss. The next day, your boss makes an announcement that the new procedure *created by your coworker* will now be the standard for the organization.
How would you respond?

- Submissively

- Aggressively

- Assertively

(Write your own example responses, *before* reviewing our comments under *Revisited*.)

———{   **HOW TO BE ASSERTIVE**   }———

1. When appropriate, establish a mutually agreeable time and place to assert your needs.
2. Describe behavior objectively, without judging or devaluing.

* Please interpret "should" here as appropriate or in your best interest. (See Tool #15.)

Example: "I felt upset and angry when you took my idea and presented it as your own."

3. Describe behavior clearly, specifying time, place, and frequency. (Not: "Why do you always do that?")

4. Express feelings calmly and directly.

5. Confine your response to the specific problem behavior, not the whole person. (Not: "You're an inconsiderate slimeball!")

6. Avoid delivering put-downs disguised as "honest feelings." (Not: "My honest feeling is that you're a total idiot!")

7. Ask for no more than one or two specific (and reasonable) changes at a time. *Example*: "I need you to listen to me without letting the phone or other people distract you."

8. Be aware of your need for approval or acceptance.

The aforementioned surprisingly workplace-relevant guidelines are adapted from Wodarski and Feit, *Adolescent Substance Abuse,* Haworth Press, 1995.

$\left[\text{THE ASSERTION SCENARIO}-\textit{REVISITED}\right]$

Obviously, saying or doing nothing in the situation described would be submissive. So would be whining about it to yourself or others. More precisely, that's manipulative.

Lashing out in anger, threatening your coworker, using profanity, or impugning his or her character (e.g., "You dishonest thief!") would be aggressive, as would be plotting revenge and malicious gossiping. (More precisely, that's passive–aggressive.)

An example of assertion would be:

1. Speaking with your coworker immediately after the meeting, expressing whatever emotion you feel, reminding your coworker that you created the procedure, inquiring whether he or she agrees and why he or she took credit, and firmly requesting that the coworker promptly go to the boss (with or without you) and state the truth of the matter.

(Be sure to give your coworker the opportunity to respond to your inquiries. For example, it is possible that he or she gave you credit for the idea and the boss was mistaken in the attribution.)

2. If your coworker denies that it really was your idea and/or declines to tell the boss the truth, assertion would then entail that you speak with the boss and simply state what really happened (along with, perhaps, expressing the emotion you feel, but without character assassination).

If you have reason to believe that your coworker would respond violently to your assertion, you might choose to skip the first step and go directly to the boss.

APPLICATION #1

1. *Review* your responses to the Self-Assessment Worksheet.

2. In what kind of *situations* are you least comfortable being assertive?

3. Resolve to *practice* assertion in those situations, even though you may feel a sense of strain initially. (You *will* feel good about yourself and, over time, you will feel more comfortable.)

APPLICATION #2

1. *Reflect* on instances in your dealings with others in which you have been aggressive (or passive–aggressive or manipulative).

2. How can you be more *assertive* in similar situations? (Tool #17 might be helpful.)

3. Resolve to *practice* assertion in similar situations, challenging that aggressive impulse.

HOW TO DEAL WITH "DIFFICULT" PEOPLE

Ultimately, everything comes down to our reaction to situations—how we choose to think about and respond to issues or people.

The following 10-point set of guidelines brings together principles and skills from this and several preceding tools:

1. ***Reframe "difficult person" into "challenging situation" to be solved by both parties.*** This is not just a euphemism. As was discussed in Tool #15, Tip #5, the words you use, even to yourself, have power. "Difficult person" dumps a negative attitude on the other individual and tends to separate you from that person. "Challenging situation" brings the two of you together on a level playing field to jointly tackle a challenge in which you both have a stake.

2. ***Take a deep breath.*** Tell yourself to calm down, or count to five. (See Tool #13.)

3. ***Allow the other person to express needs, complaints, and so on.*** After feeling listened to by you, the other person will be much more open to listening and responding favorably to your needs. And you will gain valuable information needed to address the challenge.

4. ***Utilize active listening and assertion.*** (See Tool #8.) This way, both of you will understand the other's point of view and the critical requirements for a meeting of the minds. Granted, this assumes that the other person is reasonable (and you are too). Difficult people may not seem to be reasonable, at first. However, after feeling really listened to by you, they are likely to become so. (See Defusing a Hostile Person in Tool #21.)

5. ***Turn statements into questions.*** Use the inquiry, reflective, and clarifying questions described in Tool #8. For example:

    *   "What would you like to see happen?"
    *   "My understanding is that you want . . . Is that correct?"
    *   "What else?"

6. ***Be willing to lose the battle in order to win the war.*** Focus on what is most important to you. Strive toward that end and do not get hung up on issues that are less important (but might push your buttons).

7. ***Think about the desired goal.*** Is it to see who wins or to create a win–win situation for both parties? Go for long-term fulfillment rather than short-term satisfaction of any aggressive or defensive impulse.

8. ***Recognize that old tapes begin to play in our heads.*** For example:

   • "Here she goes again."

   • "I can't deal with people like this!"

   What are some of your tapes? Such tapes undermine our self-confidence and reasonableness. When we challenge those tapes, we can choose to think, believe, and act from a position of strength. We can regain that self-confidence and refuse to be either a victim or victimizer.

9. ***Do not personalize it.*** Very often, insults apparently directed at you really are about what you represent to the other person. In general, the behavior of others says more about them—and their situation and temperament—than you and your character. Remember: Sticks and stones…

10. ***Be solution-driven, rather than right-driven.*** (In either sense of the word *right*):

    • Birthright: "You don't have the right to treat me like this!"

    • Correct: "I am right and you are wrong."

    Either may indeed be true, but compare its importance to the desired end result. After peaceably resolving the confrontation, and at a calmer moment, you can revisit the "right" issue, if it really matters.

17

Own Your Anger...Don't Let It Own You

Interpersonal effectiveness entails mastering four skills beginning with the letter A. Previous tools addressed three of those A's: Attitude, Assertion, and Active listening.

This tool unveils the fourth: Anger—how to acknowledge and experience it, process and express it, and then let it go—effectively and nonviolently. To do so, we propose "The Five Rules of Anger."

THE MISUNDERSTOOD EMOTION

In fact, anger is neither good nor bad. If you feel it, you feel it! Many people deny that they ever get angry. Further in this tool, we will talk about such denial. For now though, assume that we use this term to refer not only to rage but also to any level of disgruntlement, such as annoyance, irritation, frustration, impatience, contempt, displeasure, or even numbness—whether directed outward toward others or circumstances or inward toward oneself.

Bear this clarification in mind as you review:

The Five Rules of Anger

1. Acknowledge it
2. Experience it
3. Process it
4. Express it
5. Let it go

—[HOW ANGRY ARE YOU?   ]—

The first step to manage anger is:

The First Rule of Anger: *Acknowledge* that you are angry.

We suggest you take a minute or so to complete the following Anger Inventory Worksheet. (Feel free to substitute your own word wherever we use the terms *anger* or *angry*.)

Worksheet 17-1. How Angry Am I?

Indicate how you typically would feel in each of the following situations ... using this scale:

little or no anger		slightly irritated		moderately irritated		quite upset		extremely angry
0	—	1	—	2	—	3	—	4

Please be candid. *This is for your eyes only!*

___ 1. Someone blames me for something I didn't do.

___ 2. Someone crowds in front of me in line.

___ 3. I spill red wine on a new pair of pants and it doesn't come out.

___ 4. Someone tries to tell me what I'm thinking or feeling.

___ 5. Someone teases me or makes a joke about me.

___ 6. Someone takes credit for something I did.

___ 7. A pushy salesperson at a store won't leave me alone.

___ 8. Someone insults me and tries to make me feel bad.

___ 9. I do something nice for someone and they fail to notice it.

__ 10. After an exhausting day at work, I find my car won't start.

__ 11. A friend and I made plans for dinner and s/he doesn't show up.

__ 12. I forget to bring something from home and have to go back for it.

__ 13. Someone I'm depending on doesn't come through for me.

__ 14. I go on vacation and it rains the whole time.

__ 15. A car cuts in front of me in traffic.

____ = Total ← Now **add up** your ratings.

Adapted from *Attacking Anxiety,* Midwest Center for Stress and Anxiety, 1989.

How'd you do?

If you scored 0–15, you may be **Numb.** Either you have an unusually high tolerance level or, more likely, you are in denial or cut off from your emotions. Perhaps you think anger is bad or that you don't have a right to be angry. Pay particular attention to the second and fourth Rules of Anger ... and to the stuffing violation of the rules at the end of this tool.

Did you score 16–30? If so, you are **Mellow.** You're a relaxed person who may experience anger occasionally, but isn't controlled by it. This tool might be helpful in reinforcing the rules you already are following ... or in dealing with angry people.

Or maybe you are **Annoyed** (31–45). You're angry a bit more often than you (or others) would like. This tool can help. Pay particular attention to the third and fifth Rules of Anger ... and make sure that you are expressing your anger appropriately (the fourth rule), rather than escalating.

If you scored 46–60, you are **Furious!** You're controlled by your anger. You and others are troubled by it. You need this tool! Concentrate especially on the third rule and rigorously apply all the rules. You probably are violating the rules by escalating (see the end of this tool).

——[**EXPERIENCING ANGER**   ]——

It really is okay to feel your anger. Denying your anger or repressing it is the worst thing you can do.

The Second Rule of Anger: Let yourself *experience* it fully.

Most feelings have one-word labels. But those simple labels represent a multidimensional set of experiences:

1. **Behavioral**: in our actions and communications (both verbal and nonverbal)

2. **Emotional**: mood states like sadness, fear, rage, joy…at any intensity

3. **Mental**: those thoughts, words, and phrases that go through our heads

4. **Physical**: in the body, for example, butterflies in the stomach, headache, dizziness, clenched fists, shortness of breath, and so on

The following activity can be helpful in getting in touch with the totality of how you experience anger.

EXPERIENCING ANGER ACTIVITY

Step 1: *Remember* a time when someone or something made you angry. (If nothing comes to mind, you can refer to the situations used in the Application at the end of this tool.)

Step 2: *Describe* your symptoms—behavioral, emotional, mental, and physical—in words or phrases. Don't tell the story of the events that triggered your anger. Describe what you said and did, felt, thought, and experienced in your body.

Behavioral _____

Emotional _____

Mental _____

Physical _____

Are you surprised to discover all that's entailed whenever you experience anger (or your substitute word)? The more aware you are of that experience, the more you will be able to manage it.

PROCESSING ANGER: THREE TECHNIQUES

Although you do want to experience your anger fully, you do not want it to take you over and contaminate your actions.

Anger can be an intense emotion. You may very well feel propelled to lash out or take some other action leading to undesirable consequences. Instead...

> The Third Rule of Anger: *Process* your anger
> instead of reacting to it.

Use any or all of the following three techniques:

Technique 1: Defuse *your anger, using:*

• Breathing: Take a few slow, deep breaths and concentrate on your breathing.

• Visualization: Imagine yourself at the beach or by a lake or anywhere that makes you feel calm and peaceful.

• Self-Talk: Keep telling yourself:

"Calm down."

"I do not need to prove myself."

"I am not going to let him or her get to me."

• Try other thoughts/actions that have calmed you in the past.

Technique 2: Learn to talk about your feelings. For example:

• Involve a third party (e.g., spouse or friend) as a sounding board.

- Write an angry letter (that you don't necessarily mail).
- Use an empty chair: Imagine the person at whom you're angry is in the chair and vent.

Technique 3: Choose a constructive means to purge your tension:

- Exercise, sports, games: Expend that adrenaline nonviolently.
- Relaxation: for example, deep breathing, massage, hot bath, gentle music, or nature sounds.
- Take a time-out.
- Channel your anger into appropriate protests: for example, Mothers Against Drunk Driving (MADD). This option is great for righteous anger; use it to change the world (or your corner of it) for the better!

How do *you* process anger?

PROCESSING ANGER ACTIVITY

Step 1: *Remember* a time when someone or something made you angry. (Perhaps the same instance you used for the Experiencing Anger Activity.)

Step 2: How did you *react* to the situation?
- What *thoughts* went through your mind?
- What did you *say*, the exact words and phrases, as best as you can remember them?
- What did you *do* with your face and body? For example, did you stand up, sit down, pace, lean forward, shake your fists, fold your arms, scrunch your face?

Step 3: How did the *other* person react? Or how was the situation affected?
- At that time?
- During the days and weeks following?

Step 4: What *results* were you hoping for? Did you get them?

Step 5: How could you have *processed* your anger?

———[**EXPRESSING ANGER**   ]———

Open, honest, and direct expression can be the most effective way of managing anger.

The Fourth Rule of Anger: Whenever feasible…
express it!

Here's how to do it:
- Remind yourself that anger is a normal human emotion.
- Use open body language and direct eye contact.
- Speak in a firm voice (but not threatening).
- Do not attack or blame the other person.
- Focus on the behavior that triggered your anger.
- Use "I" statements.
- Do not drag in old issues.
- Avoid words/statements you'll regret later.

For example:
- "You just said or did…I feel angry and upset."
- **Not:** "You are an inconsiderate slimeball. I'm going to bash your . . ."

As you can see, expressing anger really is just a form of assertion. (See Tool #16.) And, as we did with assertion, we offer…

A Word of Caution

Sometimes, overtly expressing your anger is inappropriate. Hence the *whenever feasible* portion of the fourth rule.

For example, it probably would *not* be feasible when:

- Dealing with aggressive persons, especially those in authority or who are likely to react with violence (e.g., bullies).
- Dealing with a child or an especially sensitive adult who might become frightened or emotionally bruised.

- Providing performance feedback to an employee or behavior feedback to a friend. (Feedback should focus on the other person's behavior rather than on your feelings.)

- Expressing anger (at that time) would be disruptive to the situation, for example, during a group meeting, while driving, out in public, and so on. (If timing is the constraint, postpone your anger expression but don't cancel it.)

In such circumstances, you still can express your anger, but do it to a third party (or to an empty chair).

LETTING GO OF ANGER

Even if we don't immediately lash out at the person who has triggered our anger, too often we hold onto it, letting it fester and poison our interactions and well-being.

Perhaps it was not feasible to express our anger and we're still stuck with it. More likely, we simply did not utilize any of the previously described anger managing techniques, and/or we have some other motivation for clinging to our anger.

> The Fifth Rule of Anger: Give it a time limit. . .
> then *let it go!*

Ask yourself questions like:

1. Is my anger (i.e., holding on to my anger) useful?

   You may very well believe that it is useful. For example:

   - Do you find it to be energizing and mobilizing?
   - Does it make you feel powerful?
   - Does it get you results?
   - Does it get you respect? That is, you are perceived as strong and not to be trifled with.

But is there a downside? For example:

- Are those bursts of adrenaline burning you out and/or becoming addictive?
- Are you really powerful and perceived as such by others?
- Are the short-term results outweighed by a long-term backlash?
- Are you getting real respect? Or is it fear and contempt?

2. Am I angered over a situation I cannot control?

Remember the Serenity Prayer we quoted previously:

…grant me the **Serenity** to accept the things I cannot change
Courage to change the things I can
and the **Wisdom** to know the difference.

If you can change the circumstances that trigger your anger and if, all things considered, it's worth doing so, do it. Otherwise, let it go.

3. Am I staying angry at someone, hoping to make him or her feel bad?

One of our individual coaching clients spent an entire weekend angry at her husband and locking herself in their bedroom to punish him. Well, he invited some friends over to watch football games and action videos, drink beer and eat pizza, and had a grand old time.

Whom, in fact, did she punish? (Believe it or not, it wasn't until we pointed this out to her that she realized she had punished only herself.)

Even if you are effective in punishing the other person (e.g., a coworker, friend, or loved one), is that what you really want?

VIOLATING THE "RULES"

Instead of acknowledging, experiencing, processing, and expressing your anger and then letting it go, are you stuffing or escalating your anger? (Much of the following is adapted from Brigman and Goodman's *Group Counseling for School Counselors*, 2001.)

Stuffing

Stuffing is similar to the submissive alternative to assertion in Tool #16. Stuffers deny anger. They may not admit to themselves or others that they are angry. They may not be aware that they have the right to be angry.

Stuffing may not seem to have a direct or immediate negative effect, but the long-term consequences can be quite serious. Eventually, there will be some form of explosion at others or an implosion (e.g., heart attack, stroke, or depression).

Some reasons we stuff are:

1. Fear of hurting or offending someone.
2. Fear of being disliked or rejected.
3. Fear of losing control.
4. Feeling it is inappropriate.
5. It is a learned behavior (e.g., that's how our parents dealt with anger).

What about you? Why do you stuff your anger?

Escalating

Similar to the aggressive alternative to assertion in Tool #16, escalators blame and shame the person who provoked their anger. This can take the form of insults, profanity, hostility, or even sarcasm—expressed verbally or nonverbally (facial expressions and body language).

Escalating does have a direct and immediate negative effect. At a minimum, it alienates others. And it can lead to physical abuse, perpetrated by the escalator or by the person who is blamed.

Some reasons we escalate are:

1. Feeling there is no other choice.
2. To project an image of strength/power.
3. To avoid expressing underlying feelings.
4. Fear of getting close to someone.
5. It is a learned behavior (i.e., our parents, teachers, or childhood peers did it).

What about you? Why do you escalate?

APPLICATION

Step 1: *Enlist* the services of someone with whom you feel comfortable to be a listener for this practice exercise...or just use an empty chair.

Step 2: *Imagine* yourself in one of these anger-provoking situations:

Situation 1: The Demanding Supervisor

Your supervisor has been making unrealistic demands (e.g., absurd deadlines) and is verbally abusive when these demands are not met. You've had it up to here! Nothing you do is right.

Situation 2: The Denied Insurance Claim

Your health insurance provider has denied your medical insurance claim. It was for a somewhat unusual procedure to treat a serious condition of your child/spouse/self. (Select who is applicable to you.) You, and your doctor, regard the procedure as absolutely necessary. You are furious!

Situation 3: The Work/Life Crisis

Occasionally, you need to take time off, come in late, or leave a bit early in order to take care of personal business (e.g., child care, if applicable to you). Every time you do, your supervisor gives you a hard time. And now, you have been given a written warning about it. It's unfair! You're angry and frightened (you need to keep your job and to deal with your personal issues).

Step 3: *Express* your anger to the listener (or chair).

Step 4: *Reflect* back on what you said and did. If you worked with a listener, ask for feedback. To what extent did you truly express your anger, rather than engage in any of the alternatives (e.g., stuff or escalate)?

18

Rise to the Challenge of Change

This tool reveals the various manifestations and potentially devastating impact of change, including how to deal with the fear that change often triggers. You'll learn six steps to rise to the challenge.

This first decade of the new millennium is certainly "challenging times"—terrorism, war, natural disasters, and rapid change.

As trainers and coaches, we often hear clients talk about feeling that they have little control over changes in their lives. Our response is that they are probably right. As individuals, there are many occasions when we have little control over external situations or other people. But, equally true is that we do have the internal ability to choose how we react to all that is going on around us. For example, if you are distressed because you are being laid off from a job, your immediate response may be fear, worry, and even panic. Naturally! Most of us would react initially in a similar fashion to such an event.

However, the problem is not our first reaction to change. The problem is when we get stuck and find ourselves emotionally paralyzed, just when we need to be proactive. Job loss is only one example. The same reaction probably would arise when faced with any change or loss. Change usually involves feelings of sadness, grief, fear, and/or anger.

Of all these reactions, the greatest enemy of dealing with change effectively is...

THE FEAR FACTOR

Dealing with fear is one of life's greatest challenges. It tends to paralyze us. Rather than facing our fear, our impulse is to run from it, to evade, deny, escape. Some of the forms this takes include:

- Justifying present behavior: "That's the way I am!"
- Self-pity: "Nobody understands me."
- Procrastination
- Negative/skeptical attitude
- Over-analyzing and intellectualizing

Perhaps you see yourself or people you know in some of these resistance behaviors. But in order to move forward we need to face our fear. Over the years, we have gathered some nuggets of advice in this regard from a variety of sources.

The first nugget lies in the very title of Susan Jeffers's self-help book, *Feel the Fear and Do It Anyway* (1987). It's a wonderful summarization of the secret of dealing with fear.

Rather than repressing or denying that we are apprehensive, the idea is to accept that we are fearful and really feel it (analogous to the first two Rules of Anger in Tool #17). Admittedly, feeling fear is not one of the most pleasant experiences.

Then, despite any impulses to the contrary, take the action, or pursue the thought, that triggered the feelings of fear.

This wisdom is explored in greater depth through a more unusual source: science fiction. In his *Dune* novels, and the movies based on those novels, author Frank Herbert provides a Litany Against Fear:

> Fear is the mind-killer.
> Fear is the little-death that brings total obliteration.
> I will face my fear. I will permit it to pass over me and through me.
> And when it has gone past, I will turn the inner eye to see its path.
> Where the fear has gone, there will be nothing. Only I will remain.

This litany begins with acknowledging the negative consequences of giving in to fear, then a bracing of the will to face the fear and experience it ("pass over me and through me"). It concludes with the light at the end of the tunnel: "Only I will remain."

Easier said than done? Of course. But every time we feel the fear and do it anyway, our quality of life increases and it gets a bit easier.

Don't be ashamed of your fear. True courage is not fearlessness, but taking positive action in spite of fear. Only a robot—literally or figuratively—does not feel fear. If you feel fear, you know you're facing life's challenges head-on.

SIX STEPS FOR DEALING WITH CHANGE

Over the years—through research, working with others, and our own life experiences—we have learned some techniques that can help you move from reacting to change to proactively rising to its challenge.

Step 1: Recognize that change involves loss.

Even positive change involves loss, by the way. For example, a job change, whether through layoff or career advancement, means losing coworkers, familiar routines and surroundings, and the reassuring feeling of competence.

Get in touch with that loss. Experience it and put it in context with potential gains entailed in the change.

Step 2: Accept or reject the change.

If the potential gains do not outweigh the losses, you may choose to reject the change. For example, all things considered, a particular promotion may not be appropriate for you at this time in your life.

If the change is initiated by outside factors, such as a layoff or death of a loved one, the option to reject the change may not be apparent. And that option may, indeed, not be the preferred choice, but it should be considered. This may lead to a discovery of creative alternatives that would not otherwise be contemplated. For example, if you and many of your coworkers were just laid off, a healthy and productive way to reject the change, i.e., rechannel the resentment and financial worries, might be for several of you to form your own company.

Often, however, the preferred option is acceptance. This does not happen overnight. (See Step #3.) We again quote from the Serenity Prayer:

> ...grant me the **Serenity** to accept the things I cannot change
> **Courage** to change the things I can
> and the **Wisdom** to know the difference.

Step 3: Approach change as a process.

Do not expect instantaneous comfort with the change. It's like a new pair of sneakers. The old pair is worn in and comfortable. But they are ratty looking and starting to fall apart. A new pair just doesn't feel right yet, but we know it will after a few days. So we bear the temporary discomfort.

Some changes may be welcomed, such as a new job, house, or child. Some may not, such as being laid off or going on without a loved one. Either way, change can be disorienting and uncomfortable or even painful, initially. But, this too shall pass.

And typically, there are stages we move through. The following SARAH model, outlining the classic stages of grief, applies to all types of change:

Shock—numbness, confusion, disorientation
↓
Anger—or (directed inward)...depression, sadness, fear
↓
Rejection—including denial of emotional impact
↓
Acceptance—or (negatively)...resignation, that is, hopeless "acceptance"
↓
Hope—positive focus on the future

Although the manifestations, timing, and sequence vary from person to person and circumstance to circumstance, we must accept and move through whatever stage we are in, so as to reach full acceptance and hope. Otherwise, we may get stuck in one or more stages, such as bitter resignation or vacillation between anger and rejection.

Step 4: Develop a positive outlook.

Negativity is a killer, sometimes literally! Stress, brought on by negative thoughts and actions, can lead to a reduced immune system and a greater possibility of illness.

In this context of rising to the challenge of change, negative thoughts are paralyzers—telling ourselves (incorrectly) that we cannot do what we need to do.

Turn those killer thoughts into more positive—and more realistic—internal dialogue. Practice the following process (presented in Tool #15):

1. **Recognize**: Realize that you are thinking negatively.
2. **STOP**: Visualize a STOP sign and tell yourself to "Stop It!"
3. **Restate**: Reframe into a positive statement.
4. **Reward**: Even if it is simply giving yourself a pat on the back.

For example:

1. "Oh, this is impossible. I'll never be able to do this!"
2. "Stop that! That's not true."
3. "This is hard; I'm not sure yet how or when I'll succeed, but I will!"
4. "Hey! I just changed a negative into a positive. Well done!"

Initially, you'll probably miss more negative thoughts than you catch, but you'll get better and better and the process will gradually become automatic.

Have you heard the joke about the tourist in New York City who is trying to find Carnegie Hall? He approaches a street musician and asks, "How do I get to Carnegie Hall?" The answer: "Practice, practice, practice!"

Step 5: Make a plan.

Translate your positive attitude into a positive plan of action. As with any good plan, include short-term goals and timetables—what you will do and when you will do it. Review the plan regularly and revise as appropriate. (See Step #6.) Get started and take one step at a time.

Perhaps most important is to develop a support system. Surround yourself with positive people who care about you and let them in. Share the challenge you are facing, as well as your stumbles and triumphs.

One of the best-known support systems is Alcoholics Anonymous—a wonderful model for coping with change. (We have repeatedly quoted from the Serenity Prayer used by that group.) Find a sponsor—your own personal cheerleader and coach—someone to turn to when the going gets tough and with whom to share successes along the way.

Better yet would be a team of sponsors, working in coordination or separately. (A few years ago, we saw a TV news story about an entire town banding together to solve their joint unemployment problems in a very creative way: They purchased and ran the factory from the company that had shut it down.)

Perhaps your team is a religious or secular organization or consists of some combination of a family member, friend, coworker, spiritual mentor, mental health practitioner, professional life-skills coach, or training seminars.

Step 6: Allow yourself to be flexible.

Accept that life is a series of detours. The best laid plans... Many times, when we least expect it, life throws us a curve. It is not the nature of the curve so much as our ability and skill to handle detours that affect the outcome. Expect such detours. For example, you may want to develop strategies for coping with your worst-case scenario.

Don't let the detours throw you. Simply revisit your plan and revise accordingly. Remember, you can handle this!

6

Eliminating Conflict

BARRIERS TO AN EFFECTIVE WORKPLACE

In this part, we explore two of the most significant barriers to an effective workplace: harassment and violence.

Although a certain amount of healthy, creative tension can contribute to the effectiveness of a workplace, outright conflict and violence are seriously damaging.

In Tools #2 and #13, we brought to your attention the negative impact that today's increased job demands have on productivity and on job burnout. Such demands, especially when coupled with a dictatorial management style, also increase the potential for violence and conflict.

Emotional abuse, harassment, and victimization at work are major problems. This includes bullying, estimated to affect nearly one-fifth of the U.S. workforce (21 percent according to a 2001 University of Michigan survey). In September 2007, Zogby International conducted the largest scientific survey into workplace bullying for the Workplace Bullying Institute (www.bullyinginstitute.org). Among their findings:

- Bullying is four times more prevalent than illegal forms of harassment.
- In 62 percent of cases, American employers ignore allegations of bullying.

- Employers are losing an estimated 21-28 million workers because of bullying.
- 72 percent of bullies are bosses, validating the stereotype.

Some organizations are still ruled with an iron fist and decisions are made in secrecy. Harmful office gossip and rumors spread via the grapevine replace reliable information. Fear and apprehension replace trust, confidence, and loyalty. Such a dictatorial environment nurtures an atmosphere conducive to violent and harassing behavior, employees coming to believe that resistance and lashing out at authority are the only options to a sense of helpless subjugation.

Tool #19 unlocks the legal and interpersonal ramifications of harassment in the workplace: why it still occurs, its various forms, how to avoid and respond to harassment, and how to prevent it.

We open violence using two tools. In Tool #20, you'll learn about workplace violence: two prevailing myths, its true nature and scope, and how to prevent violence from scarring your workplace by using a behavioral profile of potential perpetrators and by identifying warning signs and triggering events.

Tool #21 also contends with workplace violence, but the focus is on how to handle actual violent incidents. You'll learn how to defuse a potentially violent person and how to protect yourself and others when threatened with physical violence.

Prevent All Forms of Harassment

Much of this tool originally was derived from materials provided several years ago by our fellow consultant and trainer, Ralph Parilla. Considering the subject matter, it is appropriate to point out that neither Mr. Parilla nor either of us is an attorney. None of the following should be taken as legal advice. That being said, we are very familiar with the subject: Ralph Parilla as an HR director and consultant for 40 years, Don Grimme as an Equal Employment Opportunity (EEO) director and HR manager/director for two decades, and the Grimme duo as trainers/consultants for the past 10 years.

What does harassment mean to you? When asked in our training sessions, this question elicits a wide range of responses, such as feeling bullied, disrespected, insulted, treated as an object, put down, and so on. In essence...

Harassment is aggression against another person's body or mind.

Often, harassment is an abuse of power, whether physical power or the power of position. We provide the legal definition shortly. But first...

A QUIZ

Before looking at the answers, which of the following statements do you think are true or false?

1. Harassment means demanding sexual favors from a woman.

2. Only a physical act by one employee against another constitutes sexual harassment.

3. When making a pass at a girl, "No" means "Maybe"… and "Maybe" means "Yes."

4. Sexual, racial, or ethnic bantering at work is okay as long as the other person doesn't mind.

5. A court can require a harasser to pay damages to a harassed employee.

6. Sexual visuals or objects in a workplace are okay unless someone complains about them.

7. Employee harassment is not illegal unless it is intended as harassment.

8. Giving a job promotion to a woman who has willingly participated with you in an office romance is sexual harassment.

Quiz Answers

1. *False:* Harassment means much more than demanding sexual favors from a woman:
   - Not only quid pro quo, but also intimidating, hostile, or offensive behavior.
   - Not only sexual, but also racial, ethnic, age, disability, or any other way of belittling others.
   - It also includes demanding sexual favors from a man.

2. *False:* Sexual harassment also includes nonphysical acts (e.g., verbal comments and leering) and actions by (or toward) groups.

3. *False!* In the workplace, "No" means "NO!" forever.
   And there's something else wrong with this statement. Technically, a girl is a female under the age of 18. Informally, of

course, girl often is used to refer to an adult female (e.g., girlfriend or girls' night out). But it has a belittling effect when used by men to refer to female coworkers. (It's analogous to using *boy* to refer to an African American man, although not quite as inflammatory.)

4. *False:* The other person may indeed mind the bantering, but is afraid to say anything. And others who do mind may overhear, or hear about it later.

5. *True:* A court can require the individual, not just the employer, to pay damages to the harassed employee. Some awards have been in the $100,000's!

6. *False:* The Equal Employment Opportunity Commission (EEOC) and the courts have determined that sexual visuals or objects in a workplace are not okay, even if no one objects. Examples include:

   • Portrayals of nudity, partial nudity, or sexual acts

   • Sexual devices, cartoons, jokes

   • Sexual computer images, e-mail or voicemail messages, or "adult" websites

7. *False:* It is the *effect*, not the intent.

   This opens a potential can of worms. But a standard is used: the reasonable person (or, for sexual harassment, reasonable woman). For example, let's say a male employee has a photo of his girl-friend on his desk and a female coworker objects.

   • If his girlfriend is scantily clad in the photo, a reasonable woman might very well be offended.

   • On the other hand, if the girlfriend is fully clothed but the coworker alleges that the man has lustful feelings as he looks at the photo, this would not meet the reasonable woman standard.

8. *True:* Promoting a woman who has willingly participated in an office romance with the person who promotes her is sexual harassment, for at least two reasons:

   • Was she really willing to participate, or was she afraid for her career?

- What about other qualified employees: women and men?

As you can see, there is more to workplace harassment than many people think. And it's not just harassment on the basis of sex. But let's begin with that best-known basis...

THE LAW

Harassment on the basis of sex is a violation of Title VII of the Civil Rights Act of 1964. As defined in Section 1604.11:

> Unwelcome sexual advances, requests for sexual favors, and other verbal or physical conduct of a sexual nature constitute sexual harassment when...

A key word here is *unwelcome*. Although there are exceptions (having to do with the broader context of the entire workplace), such conduct would not violate the law if it truly were welcomed and encouraged.

> 1. ... submission to such conduct is made either explicitly or implicitly a term or condition of an individual's employment.

Note the word *implicitly*. Very often harassment takes the form of subtle innuendo, rather than flat-out demands.

> 2. ... submission to or rejection of such conduct by an individual is used as the basis for employment decisions affecting such individual ...

Either of these is *quid pro quo* (i.e., "this for that") harassment. Typically, one would need to be in a position of authority to engage in it. Employment conditions or decisions include hiring, firing, promotion, salary increases, and job assignments.

If quid pro quo were the only kind of illegal harassment, there would be little need for harassment training or this tool. It's pretty straightforward and easy to eliminate . . . if you're willing to bite the bullet and fire the perpetrator, regardless of rank. But there is also the following:

> 3. ... or such conduct has the purpose or effect of unreasonably interfering with an individual's work performance or creating an intimidating, hostile, or offensive working environment.

This is *hostile environment* harassment—the broadest, most complex, confusing type. It includes the actions of nonmanagers. (And notice the word *effect.*) This is the category that is so difficult to eliminate.

——⟦ THE SHAPE OF SEXUAL HARASSMENT ⟧——

Although sexual harassment can be female to male (or even same sex), our focus is predominantly male to female harassment. It is the most common dynamic by far. Just keep in mind that men are protected also!

According to an Illinois Task Force study, 90 percent of all women surveyed think sexual harassment is a problem and 70 percent had actually been harassed. Actually, this second statistic seems conservative. Is there any woman you know who has never been harassed?

Of those who had been harassed, the forms it took are shown in Figure 19-1.

Figure 19-1. The Sexual Harassment Pyramid.

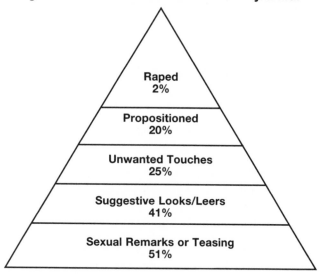

Yes, rape can be considered sexual harassment—the most extreme type of aggression against another person's body and mind. But notice the most common types; the nonphysical, suggestive looks and remarks.

THE *SECRET* TO PREVENTING SEXUAL HARASSMENT

Sexual harassment has been prohibited by law for over 40 years (i.e., the Civil Rights Act of 1964). And sexual harassment has been in the public eye for over 15 years—since Clarence Thomas and Anita Hill.

Yet harassment continues to occur in America's workplaces, resulting in big-money lawsuits and erosion of esprit de corps. A great many people are surprisingly unaware of what constitutes harassment or even that it is illegal.

We believe that the *Secret* to preventing such harassment is...

Focus on the *effect* ... not the intent!

Most employees, and some employers, don't get this. Deliberate or overt harassment is easy to deal with, and as shown in the pyramid, the least common. What trips up most employees are the subtler or unintentional forms of harassment: leering, teasing, joking, flirting, and cluelessness.

Make sure that you and your employees really grasp that "But I didn't mean anything by it!" is no defense.

THE SCOPE OF ILLEGAL HARASSMENT

Thus far, we've concentrated on sexual harassment between male and female employees. But as you saw in the Sexual Harassment Quiz, illegal harassment is much broader than that.

- Employee harassment outside the normal workplace is covered, if it is an employer-sponsored or employer-encouraged event, such as a meeting at a restaurant or bar, a business conference, a training or team-building function, and so on.

- Harassment by or of clients or vendors is covered. And don't forget your temporary employees, contractors, and part-time employees.

- Same-sex harassment is covered. Here we are not referring to sexual orientation, but rather to harassing behavior (that has sexual overtones) with someone of your own gender, for example, sexual teasing and jokes, impugning their masculinity or femininity, and so on.

- The principles of harassment also apply to race, religion, age, national origin, disability, etc., that is, any status protected by the Civil Rights Act or other federal, state, or local laws.

- Sexual orientation (e.g., homosexuality or bisexuality) is not protected under federal law. However:

    1. It is protected under many state and local laws! As a rule of thumb, if you work in a major metropolitan area, sexual orientation probably is protected. Check your state and local statutes to be certain.

    2. It is covered by many employers' policies. If your employer does business in any state, county, or city that prohibits discrimination or harassment on the basis of sexual orientation, this provision probably is included in the policy. If so, it applies to your workplace, regardless of your state or local statutes.

THE *SECRET* BASIS OF HARASSMENT

When reference is made to harassment, you think *sexual* harassment, right? During the past several years, sexual harassment charges filed with the EEOC have been averaging about 5,000 per year—not insignificant.

However, charges of *racial* harassment filed with the EEOC more than doubled during the 1990s—from 2,849 in 1991 to 6,616 in 2000. Thus far this century, these charges have plateaued at about 6,500 per year—30 percent more than sexual harassment charges!

But relatively little attention is given to this more frequent basis for harassment. Even the EEOC (in effect) has equated harassment with sexual harassment. (For example, until recently, the only reference to harassment on their website home page was sexual harassment.) And we've found that many employers have only a sexual harassment policy and conduct only sexual harassment prevention training.

Therefore, our second **Secret**...

Address *all* forms of workplace harassment.

Until you grasp this secret, your organization remains vulnerable to the most frequent basis for harassment charges.

So, what is racial harassment? According to the EEOC:

> Racial harassment is a form of race discrimination that includes racial jokes, slurs, offensive or derogatory comments, or other verbal or physical conduct based on an individual's race or color.

Although quid pro quo would not seem to be applicable here, such conduct clearly creates a hostile environment. And it's difficult to imagine a situation in which such behavior would be welcomed.

And let's not forget other bases of harassment, such as age, disability, religion…and the third most frequent basis for EEOC harassment charges: national origin (roughly 2,500 per year).

There are demeaning terms, stereotypes, and jokes for every ethnic group, or for virtually any other way of categorizing people. We've all heard them used, frequently on television, and far too often in the workplace. Many, if not most, of them violate EEO law; and all violate what should be the standard for acceptable workplace behavior: respect.

——[EXAMPLES OF HARASSMENT   ]——

Harassment can be perpetrated in endless ways. These are some examples of *verbal* harassment:

- Referring to a woman as *girl, doll, babe, honey, sweetie,* and so on
- Referring to someone's race, religion, national origin, ethnic group, age, or disability in a derogatory manner
- Referring to someone's accent or speech pattern in a derogatory manner
- Whistling at someone, catcalls, kissing sounds, howling, and so on
- Making sexual comments about a person's body or dress

- Using stereotypes, based on gender, race, sexual orientation, age, religion, and so on
- Talking about sexual preferences, fantasies, or history
- Repeatedly asking out a person who is not interested
- Telling sexual, racial, ethnic, religious jokes or stories
- Asking unwelcome personal questions about sex, race, ethnicity, religion, sexual orientation, or other inappropriate issues
- Gay bashing or using derogatory terms for gays, lesbians, bisexuals, or transsexuals
- Any other verbal behavior that has an intimidating, hostile, or offensive effect

And here are some examples of *non*verbal harassment:

- Looking at a person sexually or with hostility...or staring at someone
- Blocking a person's path...or following a person
- Giving unwanted personal gifts
- Displaying sexually suggestive, demeaning, or offensive visuals
- Making facial expressions such as winking, throwing kisses, or licking lips
- Making sexual gestures with hands or through body movements
- Mocking gays using gestures or through body movements
- Violent or aggressive conduct, pranks, or intimidation
- Physical contact other than handshakes, such as sexual/suggestive touching or unrequested back/shoulder rubs

The following are examples of behavior that is not necessarily illegal harassment, but is *potentially offensive*:

- Religious terms, such as God, Jesus, Christ, and so on. Such terms are not illegal per se, but a deeply religious person might be offended, particularly if the terms are used in anger.
- Socially offensive language:

    Bathroom activities (e.g., the "S" word)

    Bedroom activities (e.g., the "F" word)

Body parts (especially crude terms for parts usually covered
by clothing)

Even mild expletives (e.g., hell or damn) can be offensive to
some people, especially if overused

- Obscene gestures.
- Explicit noises.
- Anything that treats people other than with respect.

HOW TO AVOID HARASSING OTHERS

The aforementioned lists are far from exhaustive. However, rather than
attempting to memorize lists of specific words or actions, we recommend
following some simple guidelines. When in doubt, ask yourself any of these
five questions:

1. Would I say or do this in front of my spouse, mother, or minister/
   priest/rabbi?
2. Would I say or do this if it were to be reported in the newspaper
   or on TV?
3. Would I say or do this to a member of my same sex, race, or
   ethnic group in exactly the same way?
4. Does it follow The Golden Rule? That is, how would I feel if it
   were done to me?
5. How would I feel if this were said or done to my wife, girlfriend,
   mother, daughter, or sister?

The last one is our favorite. It transcends The Golden Rule. For example, many men would not mind if a woman were to "come on" to them.
However, they probably would mind if a man were to come on to their
daughter.

This phrasing, of course, is aimed at men and focuses on sexual harassment. Just make the appropriate substitutions for your gender or the nature
of the behavior. For example: How would I feel if this were said or done to
my son or elderly father...or about my religion, race, or ethnic group?

─[HOW TO RESPOND TO HARASSMENT]─

How would you respond to harassment?

You might be tempted to wallop the harasser. We hope, instead, that you would practice some anger management and use less violent means of expression.

In order of decreasing effectiveness, we recommend any of the following means of expressing your displeasure:

1. *Assert* yourself verbally:

   • "I am not comfortable with what you are saying/doing."

   • "Please stop that," or "I don't like that."

   • "Thank you, but no" (e.g., if asked out on a date).

2. Use the Navy's *traffic light* approach:

   • Red light   =   STOP   =   That is offensive!

   • Yellow light   =   CAUTION   =   That is borderline.

   • Green light   =   GO   =   Yes, I am comfortable.

3. Express yourself *nonverbally*:

   • Turn away or walk away.

   • Frown or shake your head.

4. Say or do *nothing* (but *report* it immediately afterward):

   • If you believe any form of confrontation would escalate matters

   • If you are a naturally shy or quiet person

─[YOUR ROLE AS A LINE MANAGER]─

Those who work in the Human Resources function have a significant role to play in harassment prevention and EEO compliance. Outside of HR, the role of the manager is no less significant, but it is more constrained.

In addition to avoiding harassment yourself, you need to *detect* and *respond* to all forms of harassment.

1. When *responding* to a harassment complaint (whether a formal complaint or informal gripe), apply the One Breath Rule:

Take one breath and call HR
(or the designated harassment official)

It is important that you not attempt to investigate and resolve harassment issues on your own. Your HR department probably will want you to expand your response role to include the following:

Listen...Assure...Document...Report.

- *Listen* to what the employee says. (See Tool #8.)
- *Assure* the employee that:

    You will treat what is said in confidence, but you must inform an appropriate HR individual.

    An investigation will be conducted promptly, maintaining as much confidentiality as possible (but the accused and/or witnesses will need to be interviewed).

    The employee will be informed of the investigation's results.

    Appropriate action will be taken. (Do not specify what that action will be.)

    There will be no retaliation against the employee for having made the complaint.

- *Document* exactly what he or she says and what you say. Take notes during your conversation. The best form for the documentation is handwritten. Indicate date, time, and location (e.g., your office). Sign it, and if the individual is willing, have the complainant sign as well.

- *Report* the conversation to your HR representative or designated harassment official—verbally and with your documentation (retain a copy or the original for yourself and provide the same to the complainant if requested). Tell the complainant that you will be making this report.

Note that assessment of the validity or severity of the complaint is not part of your role. Neither is gossip. Speak to no one other than the complainant, the designated HR/harassment representative, and investigators.

You should add gossip control to your role, in other words, caution the complainant to refrain from chatting about the matter with coworkers, and caution any individuals whom you might hear discussing the issue.

2. Line managers play an even more substantive role as *detectives*.

Be attuned to the informal subculture of your organizational unit, to the kinds of inappropriate behaviors that are tolerated, and to the symptoms displayed by those who may feel excluded or bullied.

Although utilization of the formal complaint procedure certainly should be encouraged, it is not realistic to expect it in all cases. Do not ignore informal gripes.

Pay particular attention to the odd person out, such as the one or two women in a predominantly male group, and so on. Do they feel fully accepted and part of the team?

THREE SCENARIOS

Test out your understanding of harassment with these scenarios:

SCENARIO 1: COFFEE TIME

Nancy is one of three members of a professional staff working on a project directed by Mr. Roberts. She shares an equal status with her two colleagues, both of whom are male. Whenever a meeting is scheduled, Mr. Roberts assigns the arrangements for room setup and coffee to Nancy.

1. Is this appropriate?
2. Is this illegal harassment/discrimination?
3. How could Mr. Roberts assign the arrangements for room setup and coffee?

Scenario 1 Answers

1. This is definitely not appropriate.
2. Yes; this is probably more discrimination than harassment.
3. Mr. Roberts could do it himself, have it done by an assistant, or rotate the arrangements among the three professionals on his staff.

SCENARIO 2: SAM AND DELILAH

Delilah is terribly attracted to her boss, Sam. As a ruse to be alone with him, she asks him to join her for a drink after work, supposedly to discuss a troubling work situation. After a few drinks, Delilah accepts Sam's offer to drive her home. She insists he come inside for a while. After a few more drinks, they end up spending the night together at Delilah's invitation and provocation.

1. Is Delilah's behavior illegal harassment?
2. Is Sam's behavior illegal harassment?
3. Is either Sam's or Delilah's behavior prudent?

    What could happen to Sam if Delilah were ever to allege that Sam harassed her?

    What could happen to Delilah if her coworkers hear about this evening?

Scenario 2 Answers

1. Not really. Although Delilah tricked Sam, she did not force him. As his subordinate, Delilah has no authority over Sam to abuse.
2. Not in fact. Sam did not initiate the encounter or abuse his authority.
3. Hardly! Sam is now very vulnerable and would find it difficult to prove the innocent role he played. Delilah would get a reputation as an "easy" woman, who was trying to sleep her way to the top.

SCENARIO 3: ODD MAN OUT

Lucy Leader was head of a project team at an organization just like yours. Most employees in her area had worked with her for at least two years. It was a fun group with lots of teamwork. They were very busy, knew what needed to be accomplished, and were great at putting their heads together and getting it done.

It was also a very relaxed atmosphere with a lot of bantering and joking, some of which was a bit sexual and contained a lot of innuendo. It was fun, harmless teasing and no one seemed to care. No one, that is, until Lucy hired Todd. Todd was a young man who had been able, due to his specialized expertise, to solve some problems the team had wrestled with for some time.

However, Todd seemed very serious and uncomfortable with the rest of the group. The staff consistently asked him to come with them to lunch or on breaks, but he always declined. Some employees complained that he did not belong and interfered with the overall team spirit.

Subsequently, Lucy began watching the interactions in the department more carefully to try to figure out what was going on. She noticed Tessa approach Todd several times and make remarks about how good he looked, joking and teasing a bit. Todd did not look very happy about it. Another time, during a joke told with sexual overtones, Todd was the only person who did not laugh.

1. If you were Lucy, what would you do about the situation?
2. If you were a coworker (e.g., Tessa), what would you do about the situation?
3. If you were Todd, what would you do about the situation?

Scenario 3 Answers

1. If we were in Lucy's position, we would speak first with Todd and express sympathetic concern for what appears to be his discomfort and find out more about what might be troubling him. Then we would speak with the team as a group to set new ground rules (without directly referring to Todd), supplemented by one-on-one conversations with individuals, such as Tessa. We would probably sign everyone up for some harassment training. What we would *not* do is tell Todd that he is overly sensitive or not a team player and that he should shape up or ship out.

2. If we were Todd's coworkers, upon realizing that our behavior has been making him uncomfortable, we would apologize to him and

request feedback. What changes would he like us to make in our interactions with him?

3.   If we were in Todd's position, we would assert ourselves more clearly with our coworkers and with our boss, Lucy. Legally, Todd is not required to do anything and he is entitled to file a harassment charge.

The point to this scenario is that just because no one complained about these behaviors in the past, does not mean that they are appropriate, or even legal, in today's workplace. They just hadn't been caught until Todd arrived.

─┌ TEN TIPS TO PROTECT AGAINST HARASSMENT CHARGES ┐─

In Appendix A, we provide ten tips to prevent harassment and discrimination in the workplace that are geared to the organization as a whole. All leaders should be aware of these tips and provide support as needed; however, many of them need to be executed by senior officials and/or the HR department.

APPLICATION

1.   Think about some of the interpersonal behaviors engaged in by your employees, both in the workplace and at lunch or after-hours get-togethers.

2.   Have there been instances that you now realize may be considered harassment: demeaning words, jokes, suggestive or hostile comments, touching or looks, and so on?

3.   What can you do to begin turning that behavior around? With whom can (or should) you discuss your observations and intended actions?

Prevent Workplace Violence

9/11 was a huge wake-up call for Americans to the danger of organized terrorism. But most of us have yet to wake up to what may be an even greater danger, certainly a more chronic one, that of unorganized terrorism—those so-called random acts of violence that have been plaguing this nation, and especially this nation, for years.

In this context, we recommend one of the best books on protection from violence, not only in the workplace but also in every aspect of our lives: *The Gift of Fear* by Gavin de Becker.

In his introduction, de Becker observes that:

> In a [recent] two-year period, more Americans died from gunshot wounds . . . than were killed during the entire Vietnam War. In contrast, in all of Japan, . . . the number of young men shot to death in a year is equal to the number killed in New York City in a single busy weekend.

We're not sure why de Becker chose to focus on young men. But his particular comparisons have special meaning for one of the authors, when he was a young man. You see, the closest that Don Grimme ever came to being violently killed was not during his military service in Vietnam, but one year later while working for an employment agency on the top floor of an office building in the heart of midtown Manhattan. He'll tell his story in Tool #21.

This tool unlocks how to prevent violent incidents from ever occurring and covers:

* Two prevailing myths about workplace violence
* The true nature and scope of workplace violence
* How to prevent violence from scarring your workplace by using a behavioral profile of potential perpetrators and by identifying the warning signs and triggering events of violence

In the next tool, you'll learn how to protect yourself and others when faced with a violent situation.

WORKPLACE VIOLENCE IS ON THE UPSWING!

This was the headline of a July 2005 *HR Magazine* article, which asserted:

> Workplace violence...increased over the past two years despite federal statistics to the contrary.

Why the discrepancy between the magazine's assertion and the government stats? Because they are looking at different phenomena.

Federal statistics focus on physical attacks, which have declined somewhat during the past several years, especially homicides. (This assumes that terrorist attacks like 9/11 are not included. Typically, 9/11 is not thought of as workplace violence. It could be, however. The World Trade Center and the Pentagon certainly were workplaces.)

The Risk Control Strategies survey used by the *HR Magazine* article focuses on other forms of violence:

* Verbal and electronic threats
* Sexual harassment

- Malicious downloading of viruses

As you will see, these definitely have been on the increase.

TWO MYTHS

During the years we have been consulting on this issue, we have observed two prevailing myths regarding workplace violence.

Myth 1: It can't happen here.

We call this myth "The Ostrich Syndrome." If the wave of violence over the past several years has demonstrated anything, it is that violence can strike at any time, in any community, and in any workplace.

The era of workplace violence began in 1986, when postal worker Patrick Sherrill murdered 14 coworkers in Edmund, Oklahoma. At the time, it was the third worst mass murder in U.S. history. But it's not just post offices.

More recently, we've seen that violence can assault a high school in Littleton, Colorado, two day-trading firms in Atlanta, Xerox in Honolulu, a small software firm outside of Boston, Lockheed Martin in Mississippi, and a university in rural Virginia (the worst civilian gun massacre in U.S. history).

But are these just isolated incidents? Let's take a look:

- The Centers for Disease Control have declared workplace violence to be at epidemic levels.
- The U.S. Department of Justice proclaimed the workplace to be the most dangerous place to be in America.
- In fact, one in four workers are attacked, threatened, or harassed every year.

And the toll of this violence? Costs related to workplace violence have risen a staggering 2,881 percent from $4.2 billion in 1992 to $121 billion in 2002.

All right, that's the bad news. The good news is revealed when we expose:

Myth 2: It can't be prevented.

Balderdash! In fact, 99 percent of incidents have clear warning signs, if you know what to look for.

The extensive news reports of the massacre at Virginia Tech in 2007 did a good job identifying Seung-Hui Cho's warning signs. In the Resource Guide for this tool, we include a reference to a comprehensive consolidation of those warning signs found in Wikipedia.org; and we use Cho as one of our examples throughout this tool. Let's look now at another example.

Within just hours of the Lockheed Martin murders in Mississippi in 2003, reporters learned that the gunman had had frequent conflicts with managers and coworkers. He was a known racist and talked about killing people.

You do not have to be a forensic psychologist to detect warning signs like these.

We'll explore the warning signs of violence in much greater depth shortly. But first...

A QUIZ

1. True or False: Domestic violence has little impact on workplace violence.

2. True or False: Homicide is the leading cause of on-the-job death for women.

3. Each year the number of victims of workplace violence is about: (a) 50,000 (b) 100,000 (c) 500,000 (d) 1 million

4. In the workplace, simple assaults outnumber homicides by a factor of: (a) 10 to 1 (b) 50 to 1 (c) 100 to 1 (d) 600 to 1

5. The person most likely to attack someone in the workplace would be a: (a) customer (b) stranger (c) coworker (d) boss (e) former employee

THE NATURE AND SCOPE OF WORKPLACE VIOLENCE

We use the format of the quiz to present the true nature and scope of workplace violence. Here are the correct answers.

1. **False.** In fact, domestic violence spillover is the fastest growing category of physical workplace violence.

2. **True.** Homicide is the leading cause of on-the-job death for women. And it is the second leading cause for men.

3. **(d)** There are *1 million* victims of workplace violence annually. And this is only physical violence. Some estimates are as high as 2 million. The problem with getting a more accurate number is that most nonlethal workplace violence is never reported to the police. But, of course, not all of this violence is homicide.

4. **(d)** In the workplace, simple assaults outnumber homicides by a factor of *600 to 1*.

Figure 20-1. The Iceberg of Workplace Violence.

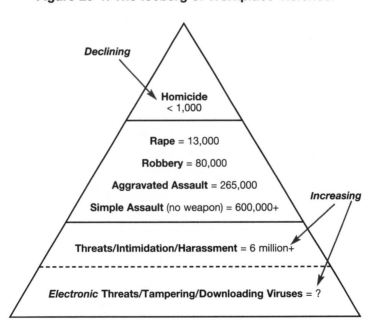

The point here is that there are fewer than 1,000 workplace homicides each year and homicides have been declining during the past few years. However, these homicides, which understandably receive all the media coverage, are only the tip of the total workplace violence iceberg, which also includes rapes, robberies, and assaults, both with and without a weapon. And notice that the incidence of verbal violence is at least six times that of physical violence.

Also, as stated previously, the newest form of workplace violence is electronic: e-mail threats, computer tampering, and malicious downloading of viruses—all very much on the increase.

5. (a) If you thought the person most likely to attack someone in the workplace would be a former employee or coworker, that's understandable, based on press coverage.

   However, the correct answer is *customer*—at about 44 percent. For example, perpetrator Mark Barton was a customer, not an employee, of those Atlanta day-trading firms. And as a student, Seung-Hui Cho was a customer of Virginia Tech.

   You would get partial credit if you answered stranger, which is the most likely perpetrator of workplace homicides...and, at 24 percent, second only to customers for total workplace violence.

   Former employees cause only 3 percent of workplace attacks. Current employees, that is, coworkers, are a more significant threat at 20 percent. And bosses are responsible for 7 percent of all physical workplace violence.

   Bear in mind, however, that these statistics are based on reported incidents. As we mentioned, most employee fistfights and shovings go unreported.

─┤   WHO'S AT RISK?   ├─

Men certainly are at risk (twice as likely as women), but remember that murder is the number one cause of workplace death for women. Supervisors and managers are also at risk, for example, during a recent 10-

year period, employee–boss murders doubled. Occupations like law enforcement officer, taxi driver, health care, and retail worker...and departments like security, safety, and HR are especially at risk. In general, any job that involves extensive contact with the public or with employees is at risk of workplace violence.

These are highlights of those most vulnerable to lethal violence. Anyone is vulnerable to nonlethal violence.

─┤ PREDICTING WORKPLACE VIOLENCE ├─

Since the phrase "going postal" is often uttered when speaking about incidents of workplace violence, we created the formula or acronym, POSTAL, to organize the clues that are available to identify a potential workplace violence perpetrator.

Formula for Workplace Violence.

POSTAL

Profile (previous behavioral characteristics)

+

Observable Warning Signs (current behavior)

+

Shotgun (or other weapon access/familiarity)

+

Triggering Event(s)

=

Always
Lethal

By **P**rofile, we mean behavioral characteristics, not racial profiling. In this case, previous behavior. Observable Warning Signs also are behavioral, but now the focus is current behavior. Shotgun is access to and familiarity with any weapon (but we needed an "S" for the acronym). Triggering Event is that last straw, or set of straws, that sets off the violence-prone individual.

Note: Shotgun is not required for nonlethal violence.

Each of these elements is illustrated in the following classic case study (by Michael D. Kelleher in *New Arenas for Violence*) of the first person to "go postal." See if you can spot them.

CLASSIC CASE STUDY: "GOING POSTAL"

In August 1986, 44-year-old postal employee, Patrick Sherrill, dressed in his usual blue uniform and carrying a mailbag over his shoulder walked into the U.S. Post Office in Edmond, Oklahoma. On this day, though, inside his mail pouch were two loaded .45-caliber pistols he had checked out from the National Guard Armory (where he was a member of the marksmanship team). He also carried over 300 rounds of ammunition and a .22-caliber handgun, which was his own property.

Sherrill said nothing as he immediately walked up to the shift supervisor and shot him in the chest. Still silent, Sherrill stalked more victims throughout the post office. His rampage lasted for only 10 minutes, but during that time, he managed to murder 13 more employees (wounding six others). In a final act of violence, Sherrill turned one of the guns on himself and committed suicide.

This horrific crime inaugurated the era of the violent workplace in the press and the minds of many Americans. At the time, it was the third worst mass murder in American history.

Why did he do it? This was a man a onetime neighbor described as shy and gentle who liked the words "thank you" and "please." Speculation ranged from post-traumatic syndrome to a poor performance review. A few employees said they thought Sherrill's murderous rampage was an act of revenge.

The morning before the murders, Sherrill had met with the shift supervisor and senior supervisor to discuss his work performance. It is believed that the senior supervisor threatened to terminate Sherrill. He was scheduled to meet with his supervisor the morning of the murders to discuss performance issues.

Sherrill had been a Marine sharpshooter and Vietnam War veteran. Before his job as letter carrier, he held a number of short-term jobs as file clerk, stockroom worker, and bicycle repairman. Throughout his life, Sherrill held a strong fascination for weapons and was highly proficient in their use. He was in a position to acquire weapons quickly and easily.

Patrick Sherrill had lived on the same street for 20 years. His neighbors referred to him as "Crazy Pat" because of his strange behavior in the neighborhood. He would, at times, mow his lawn at midnight, peer into neighbor's windows while wearing combat fatigues, or tie up neighborhood dogs with bailing wire. He was, by many neighborhood accounts, a loner and a strange individual. Sherrill had lived with his mother all his life until her death in 1974; after that he lived alone.

At work, people viewed Sherrill as often angry and frequently depressed. Coworkers perceived him as a problem employee. They said he preferred his own company to normal workplace socialization. Some described him as a habitual complainer and a consistent nonperformer. He was enigmatic and not well understood by anyone who knew him. This would later prove to be the common profile for a potentially violent employee.

SOURCE: *New Arenas for Violence: Homicide in the American Workplace* by Michael D. Kelleher, Copyright © 1996. Greenwood Publishing Group, Inc., Westport, CT.

Let's start with the first element of POSTAL: the **P**rofile of a potential workplace violence perpetrator…

PROFILE

Before beginning the behavioral profile, a brief word on the demographic profile. Notice that Patrick Sherrill was a 44-year-old man. Indeed, middle-aged male is the stereotype and a somewhat accurate one. The vast majority of perpetrators of physical workplace violence (not necessarily verbal or electronic violence) are male, and many are middle-aged.

Our main reason for commenting on the age aspect of the profile is that it is the opposite of the street crime profile. However, there are far too many exceptions for it to be useful. For example, Seung-Hui Cho of Virginia Tech was in his early twenties and Harris and Klebold of Columbine were still in their teens.

Note: The similarities between workplace violence and school violence are greater than the differences; and high schools and universities are workplaces. Because of their notoriety, we include Cho, Harris, and Klebold among our examples illustrating the POSTAL elements.

All workplace violence perpetrators previously displayed several of the following six behavioral characteristics:

1. ***Previous history of violence.*** Our first factor is the single most significant. This history of violence usually is toward those most vulnerable. For example, Sherrill tied up neighborhood dogs with bailing wire. Harris of Columbine tortured animals.

   But it could be women or children. Barton murdered his wife and children just before his day-trading massacre and he was suspected by the police of having murdered his first wife. Wife beaters and child abusers are prime candidates for workplace violence.

   This could also include violent artistic expression, for example, as in the two plays written by Virginia Tech's Cho and the video produced by Harris and Klebold of Columbine.

2. ***Loner.*** Typically, perpetrators are withdrawn and socially isolated. For example, Sherrill lived with his mother until her death, then lived alone during the last 12 years of his life. Harris and Klebold weren't even members of the anticlique Trenchcoat Mafia; they were only on its fringes. And Cho certainly was a loner.

   • A loner also feels nobody listens to him...no one is on his side.

   • A loner views change with fear and suspicion and as a personal affront.

3. ***Emotional problems.***

   • Substance abuse or other self-destructive behavior; not an issue for Sherrill, but this usually is associated with nonlethal violence

   • Unresolved mental health problems (e.g., depression) that were evidenced by Sherrill, Cho, and the boys of Columbine, and are consistent with the lethal violence profile

   • Elevated frustration level and temper-control difficulties—also an issue for Sherrill

- Low self-esteem where one's sense of worth is tied to the job, a group, or a person (remember this when we talk about Obsessions and Triggering Events)

4. *Career frustration.* This often is reflected in either significant tenure on the same job or migratory job history. In Sherrill's case, it was migratory. Other examples of career frustration include Barton's losses in the stock market and Harris of Columbine, who had just been rejected by the Air Force Academy.

5. *Antagonistic relationship with others.* A person prone to violence often:

   - Externalizes blame for life's disappointments

   - Is disgruntled and has disdain for authority, for example, Sherrill was a habitual complainer

   - Threatens, intimidates, or harasses others

   - Has interpersonal problems and conflicts

6. *Obsession.* Our final profile attribute is the second most significant. In Sherrill's case, it certainly included obsession with weapons and other acts of violence. But it also includes:

   - Zealotry, whether political, religious, or racial, for example, the Lockheed Martin perpetrator

   - A romantic or sexual obsession, for example, Cho and his stalking incidents

   - The job itself (Keep this one in mind when we talk about Triggering Events.)

   - Even an extreme concern with neatness and order

A WORD OF CAUTION

It's important to bear in mind, however, that having any one or even two of these characteristics does not mean someone will become violent. (A history of violence and some of the obsessions are exceptions.)

There are millions of people who are frustrated in their careers, suffer from depression or anxiety, or are introverts who will never commit violence. It's the profile characteristics as a total picture that distinguishes the potential workplace violence perpetrator. As Dr. Lynne McClure states in her book *Risky Business* (1996):

> ... in combination, they form patterns that signal lack of responsibility, lack of self-management, and lack of concern for others—patterns which, under intense situations, easily increase the potential for violence.

─┤   APPLYING THE PROFILE   ├─

This is all very interesting, but how can you use this information as a workplace leader? You can be on the alert for attributes in the Profile as you interact with coworkers, review personnel files and, especially...

During the Hiring Process

Look for signs of the Profile as you conduct:

- Critical reviews of information on résumés and applications
- In-depth interviews
- Validated drug and psychological testing
- Background checks (employment, criminal, credit, and so on)

(See also the Employee-Selection Techniques portion of Appendix B.)
Should you refuse to hire someone who, for example, has had a mental health problem (and thereby violate ADA regulations)? No, of course not. But if you also detect other factors, certainly proceed with caution and investigate further.

That's the Profile. For your existing workforce, and when dealing with outsiders, we turn to the...

─┤   OBSERVABLE WARNING SIGNS   ├─

These warning signs, which can be newly acquired negative traits, parallel and overlap the Profile, but now we are focusing on current behavior. So, instead of a previous history of violence, our first warning sign is observed...

1. **Violent and threatening behavior.** For Sherrill, it was tying up neighborhood dogs with bailing wire and a strong fascination with weapons.

    In general, violent and threatening behavior may include:

    *   Destruction of property or threats of sabotage.
    *   Disregard for the safety of others or violation of safety procedures.
    *   Threats, intimidation, or bullying, for example, Cho and the boys of Columbine (as both perpetrators and victims).
    *   Violence against a family member, for example, Barton.
    *   Stalking or harassing others. Cho was involved in at least three stalking incidents, the first occurring 18 months prior to his rampage. Also, he placed harassing phone calls to his roommate and took cell phone pictures of female students' legs under their desks.

2. **Strange behavior.** Sherrill's neighbors noted his strange behavior in the neighborhood: mowing his lawn at midnight and peering into neighbor's windows while wearing combat fatigues. His coworkers said he preferred his own company and described him as enigmatic. Cho was known as the question-mark kid. He had an imaginary girlfriend who lived in outer space.

    In general, strange behavior may include:

    *   Becoming reclusive, for example, a sudden withdrawal from friends or acquaintances
    *   Poor personal hygiene or a deteriorating and unkempt appearance
    *   Inappropriate dress, for example, Cho never took off his sunglasses, even indoors
    *   Bizarre or paranoid behavior
    *   Erratic behavior or an extreme change in behavior

3. **Emotional problems.** For example, Sherrill was often angry and frequently depressed. A district court found Cho to be "an imminent danger to himself as a result of mental illness."

Professors described him as insecure and depressed, as were
the boys of Columbine. In general, emotional problems may
include:

- Drug or alcohol abuse
- Appearing to be under unusual stress; signs of depression
  or despondence
- Inappropriate emotional display, for example, screaming,
  explosive outbursts, rage, and/or crying

4. ***Performance problems.*** Sherrill's coworkers perceived him as a
   problem employee and a consistent nonperformer. Virginia Tech
   declined to divulge details about Cho's academic record, but his
   mother was increasingly concerned about his inattention to
   classwork and his time spent out of the classroom. In general,
   performance problems may include:

   - Inability to concentrate; decreased energy or focus
   - Deteriorating work performance
   - Attendance or tardiness problems
   - Increased need for supervision; coworkers have to pick
     up the slack

5. ***Interpersonal problems.*** Cho was described as awkward and
   lonely, arrogant and obnoxious, timid, dorky and pushy. Sherrill
   was a habitual complainer. Interpersonal problems may include:

   - Numerous conflicts with supervisors and other employees
   - Hypersensitivity or extreme suspiciousness
   - Resentment and frustration
   - Exaggerated perceptions of injustice

6. ***At the end of his rope.*** The last warning sign on our list is also
   the last warning sign a potential perpetrator probably will display.
   For example:

   - Has a plan to solve all problems. What do you think that
     plan might entail?
   - Indicators of impending suicide (e.g., selling property,
     closing credit union account).
   - Other indications of extreme desperation, marital discord,
     financial distress, and so on.

Cho purchased guns in the two months preceding his rampage, spent time at a local target range, began working out at the gym, and shaved his head military style. Also, there was the media package Cho sent to NBC News. (It was not received until after the massacre, of course, but wouldn't his roommates have had some awareness of its preparation?)

SHOTGUN

Shotgun simply represents access to and familiarity with weapons—not only shotguns but also handguns, rifles, explosives, and knives...or box cutters—also martial arts training.

Sherrill certainly had this; and Cho and the boys of Columbine acquired it.

Shotgun is not a warning sign. Hunters and gun collectors are not more likely to commit workplace violence, unless they are obsessed with their guns. The relevance of Shotgun in the formula is that without access to and familiarity with weapons, workplace violence probably will not be lethal.

TRIGGERING EVENT(S)

The Triggering Event is the last straw, or set of straws, experienced by the perpetrator as no way out, no more options. This could be:

1. *Job/career related.* Sherrill's rampage appeared to be an act of revenge for a poor performance review. The morning before the murders, his senior supervisor threatened to terminate Sherrill and he was scheduled to meet with his immediate supervisor the morning of the murders to discuss performance issues. Remember the significance of obsession with the job in the Profile.

   But job- or career-related events, such as being disciplined, fired, or even criticized, are only one type. It can also be...

2. *Institutional.* For example, foreclosure on a mortgage, bankruptcy, a restraining order, or custody hearing.

3. *Personal crisis.* For example, divorce, death in the family, or a

failed or spurned romance—as it may have been for Harris, whose girlfriend had recently broken up with him.

It may even be a...

4. **Benchmark date**. For example, turning 40 or a 10-year company anniversary...and feeling he is going nowhere in life. Or the anniversary of some other event that is significant to the individual.

   The Columbine massacre occurred on April 20. Do you know whose birthday that is? Adolf Hitler. Not a date most of us celebrate or even know, but significant to those two budding neo-Nazis.

All of us have experienced one or more of the aforementioned unpleasant events in our lives, which probably triggered negative feelings. Such events may trigger violence in those already primed for it, in other words, they fit the Profile and/or display the Observable Warning Signs.

These events would tend to shake anyone's sense of balance, at least temporarily. A violence-prone person already is unbalanced. The triggering event pushes him over the edge.

APPLYING POSTAL TO PREVENT WORKPLACE VIOLENCE

Look for the Observable Warning Signs and Triggering Events as you:

- Deal with your employees on a day-to-day basis
- Interact with customers and observe strangers

How you handle individuals who exhibit the warning signs will vary considerably depending on the severity and situation. At a minimum, sit down and listen to the troubled individual.

The one absolute:

Never ignore!

In the words of the husband of one of the victims at Lockheed Martin:

Obviously, he was a sick guy. I wish somebody had given him some help…before he destroyed my life and my kids' life.

Our prescription for preventing employee-initiated violence includes:

- Benevolent, motivational management practices (some organizations are breeding grounds for violence)
- Appropriate use of counseling, EAP, disciplinary action, and/or law enforcement
- Employee and management training—all employees need to know about the warning signs (and the anger-defusing techniques covered in the next tool)
- Sound security measures, which, at a minimum, eliminate Shotgun from the equation
- A zero-tolerance violence policy, effectively communicated and enforced

A clarification about zero tolerance: This term is often used to mean applying the same severe punishment for even minor offenses. That is not what we mean. Minor offenses and potential red flags should never be tolerated or ignored, but your response to them should be proportional and appropriate.

This tool's goal has been to prevent violence from ever occurring at your workplace, at least as initiated by employees. Our final tool shows you how to deal with outsiders and with actual violent incidents.

21

Defuse and Protect

This tool, like Tool #20, unlocks workplace violence, but our focus now is on how to handle actual or potentially violent incidents. You'll learn:

- How to defuse hostile, potentially violent employees and customers
- How to protect yourself and others when threatened with actual violence
- How to safely discipline or terminate an employee

DEFUSING A HOSTILE COWORKER OR CUSTOMER

The POSTAL formula and its applications are intended to prevent violence. But what can you do when confronted with a hostile, potentially violent employee or outsider? Well, we have an acronym for that as well.

Let's see if you can guess what it is. In a sense, "postal" has become our metaphor for the potential workplace violence perpetrator. Well, what is the postal carrier's traditional nemesis? That's right…

DOGS

By which we mean:

Defusing **O**f **G**rievance = **S**afety

Visualize a big balloon that's about to explode. Instead of puncturing the balloon with confrontation, you want to *gradually* deflate the balloon.

You can do this by confirming a person's perspective, without necessarily agreeing with it.

We learned the following six-point guideline from hostage negotiator Larry Chavez of Critical Incident Associates:

1. **Understand the mindset of the hostile person.** He has a compelling need to communicate his grievance. Even if he's wrong, his perceptions are real to him. Usually the person just wants fairness.

   On the other hand, he probably is not reasonable, at least initially. Don't expect calm rationality or attempt to engage in problem solving too early in the process.

   A person in crisis will only respond favorably to someone who is believed to be understanding, willing to listen, worthy of respect, and nonthreatening. Most important—preserve the individual's dignity! Never belittle, embarrass, or verbally attack a hostile person (or any person).

2. **Avoid confrontation.** Instead, have as your goal building trust and providing help. Remain calm and create a relaxed environment. Make sure you are courteous and respectful, patient and reasonable, open and honest.

   Avoid:
   - Challenging body language (e.g., crossed arms, pointing fingers, jaw thrust forward)
   - Getting "in his face," respect personal space (at least three feet away)
   - Anger words (e.g., profanity, insults, etc.), over-familiarity, or extreme formality
   - Hostile paraverbals (how you say what you say)—your tone, volume, and speed

3. ***Allow a total airing of the grievance without comment.*** Permit verbal venting or ranting, but set and enforce reasonable limits. Be empathetic and tune in to the person's feelings, without judging. Make eye contact, but do not stare.

   And ignore challenges and insults. Do not take it personally; redirect attention to the real issue.

4. ***Practice active listening.*** (See Tool #8.)
   - Stop what you are doing and give him your full attention.
   - Use silence. Do not rush in to attempt to complete his thoughts.
   - Collect the facts on the problem: who, what, and when (leave why for later).
   - Listen to what is really being said. What does he want you to understand?
   - Use reflective questioning to confirm that you've really heard him.
   - Ask clarifying and open-ended questions to assist him in getting it all off his chest.

5. ***Allow the aggrieved party to suggest a solution.*** Thus far, your primary goal has been to de-escalate the immediate situation. Now that the person has calmed down, he probably will be more open to a rational discussion of his issues. You're now ready to begin problem solving.

   Use inquiry to define the problem and to solicit his suggestions. (See Tool #8.) He will more readily agree to what happens next if he helped formulate it. And you may be surprised by how reasonable his suggestions now are.

   Assure him you'll act on any injustices he has suffered and carry out your commitments.

6. ***Move toward a win-win resolution.*** Offer something and have him do likewise. For example, offer to take specific actions to redress his grievance and request that he refrain from future outbursts.

   With the person's permission, call in additional resources, for example, your boss, his boss, an HR representative, your EAP, even a security guard or the police, if warranted. (Yes, he may very well agree to this. Now that he is calmed and has regained his reason, he may realize that his actions have violated your policy or the law, and his own sense of honor.)

APPLICATION

Step 1: *Enlist* the services of someone with whom you feel comfortable to play an angry or upset person for this practice activity.

Step 2: Have that person *choose* one of the situations from the Application at the end of Tool #17 or remember a time when he or she was upset, explain the situation to you, and then *act* it out.

Step 3: *Apply* the defusing guidelines and attempt to talk the person down. Better yet, listen the person down. Take whatever time is needed.

Step 4: *Reflect* on what happened. Ask for feedback from your partner.

- What worked? For example, what did you say or do that calmed the person and gained his or her trust?
- What did not work as well? For example, what did you say or do that aggravated the situation or caused a stalemate at any point?

COPING WITH SOMEONE THREATENING YOU WITH A WEAPON

You have learned how to de-escalate a potentially violent person. But what can you do when faced with actual violence, specifically when you are threatened with a weapon?

Larry Chavez has provided a six-point guideline for this, as well:

1. **Quietly signal for help.** Use a duress alarm system (e.g., a panic button or a code word). And have someone *else* call 911. In this regard, here is Don's story of his brush with violence...

In the fall of 1972, I was working for an employment agency on the top floor of an office building in the heart of midtown Manhattan. At 4:30 p.m. on a Friday afternoon, two gunmen walked off the elevator into the agency and proceeded to hold us up.

The first I became aware of it was when I looked up from a phone call I was on to see a gun pointed at my head. The gunman told me to "Shut up and put down the phone, you @#$%!"

My first impression, believe it or not, was that it was a toy gun. I said, "Go away; don't bother me." **Note:** That is **not** a good defusing technique!

Fortunately, my three coworkers in that office area were not as clueless as I. They said, "Don, this is serious. Put down the phone." I did and we were all tied up.

We've inserted my story here, since, obviously, I was not in a position to pick up the phone again and dial 911. Fortunately, a coworker in another office area down the hall heard the commotion and told the person with whom she was speaking on the phone to "Call the police. I think we're being held up!"

Twenty minutes later, two policemen entered our offices with their guns holstered to investigate a vague report. There was a gunfight in the hallway. We all scurried under our desks. One of the gunmen was killed. The other, after pursuit in a stairwell, was arrested. Fortunately, neither the policemen nor any of us employees were injured.

2. ***Keep your cool; don't aggravate his rage***. Maintain eye contact, but do not stare. Project calmness, although you may not be feeling calm. Do not raise your own voice.

   Use the body language and phrasing described in the defusing guidelines.

3. ***Stall for time and personalize***. Create and sustain conversation, unless instructed otherwise by the perpetrator (as Don was). Keep repeating your name. Talk about your family. Connect as a fellow person.

Use the listening and questioning techniques from less escalated situations, to the extent possible.

4. **Negotiate.** Try to get as many little yeses from the perpetrator as possible to prepare for Step #6. Start with basic requests, such as "Is it okay if I take a deep breath?" Request permission to take at least three steps away from the perpetrator.

5. **Respect the weapon, but focus on the person holding it.** Follow the instructions of the person with the weapon. (Do as we say, not as Don did.)

   Do not risk harm to yourself or others.

   Never attempt to disarm or accept a weapon from the person in question. Why do you think we say to not accept a weapon, even if offered voluntarily?

   If you are holding the weapon, it is still in play as a visible source of violence. And if someone else has called the police and they arrive on the scene, *you* will be perceived as the perpetrator.

   Instead, request that he place any weapons in a neutral location while you talk.

6. **Look for opportunities for getting yourself and others to safety.** For example, ask if uninvolved parties may leave the area—one of the significant negotiations toward which you've being building.

   Stay on the alert for a safe chance to escape. In Don's story, they scrambled under their desks once the gunfire started.

TIPS FOR SAFELY DISCIPLINING OR TERMINATING AN EMPLOYEE

Tip #1: Coordinate your decision and communications with an objective and consistent third party, such as HR.

Tip #2: Preserve the involved employee's dignity. Never insult or demean the individual, even if he or she has violated policy or been a thorn in your side.

Tip #3: Whenever there is the slightest concern about a terminated employee becoming volatile:

- Have a second person present at the meeting. When terminating a male employee, at least one of the two people present should be male (preferably with a strong physical presence).

- Conduct the meeting near an exit and away from other employees.

- Do not allow the employee to return to the work area, at least without a physically strong escort.

- Discourage/prohibit the employee from returning to any of your work sites.

Tip #4: When terminating a contract employee, confirm that the contract agency has effectively communicated the termination. Otherwise, assume full responsibility for doing so, safely.

"WHAT WOULD YOU DO IF" SCENARIOS

Test out your understanding of violence prevention and defusing principles in the following scenarios. In each case, what would you do?

SCENARIO 1: THE STUBBORN SMOKER

You attempt to enforce the no-smoking rule in the employee break area. Smoky is a long-term employee who says, "I'll smoke where I want, when I want." He flips the cigarette butt at you and lights up again.

SCENARIO 2: THE DRUNKEN CONTRACTORS

Several individuals on a contractor crew drink their lunch.

Scenario 2A: Upon returning from lunch, the contractors are stopped from entering the facility by the security officer at the employee entrance. Shouting, verbal insults, and pushing ensue.

Scenario 2B: The contractors are not stopped at the employee entrance and they return to work in the Machine Room. An argument ensues in the area of their job boxes, providing abundant tools as potential weapons.

SCENARIO 3: THE JEALOUS HUSBAND

A married couple work different shifts. Suspicious Sam works the second shift and Adulterous Adel works the first shift. Convinced that Adel is having an affair with one of her coworkers, Romeo, during the hours that Sam works, Sam takes a day off and comes to sit in the parking lot, intending to confront Adel and Romeo.

SCENARIO 4: I'M FIRED?!

You have been asked to stand by during a termination. The HR representative, Penny Personnel, believes that the terminated employee, Hostile Harry, may react violently. And in fact he does—shouting and throwing things around Penny's office, next door to where you are waiting.

——[TEN STEPS TO MANAGE WORKPLACE VIOLENCE]——

In Appendix B, we outline ten steps the organization as a whole should take to manage workplace violence. All leaders should be aware of them and provide support as needed, but many of the steps need to be executed by senior officials and/or the HR department.

AFTERWORD

We hope this book has been and will continue to be a valuable resource to you. However, the printed word can go only so far in enabling learning and personal growth. We suggest three other venues to supplement this:

1. Our complimentary *e-newsletter*, the archive of which is located online at http://www.WorkplacePeopleSolutions.com. Portions of most of the 21 tools originally were published here. Its advantage is that, for the past few years, key points are illustrated by color photos and illustrations, and hyperlinks to other relevant Web pages are provided. Visit our main Web site at http://www.GHR-Training.com to subscribe...or visit our topic-specific sites at http://www.Employee-Retention-HQ.com and http://www.Workplace-Violence-HQ.com for more on those subjects.

2. We welcome your correspondence as a means to *discuss* any of the issues or points made in this book. Write to us at Solutions@ GHR-Training.com. We will respond personally (unless and until we become overwhelmed).

3. Live, interactive *training* is the single most effective means of acquiring knowledge, insight, and skills. And that is our specialty. The Grimmes deliver training workshops and keynote presentations on all of the topics addressed in this book. We've done this with organizations of every size and in every sector of the economy. Contact us at (954) 720–1512 or Solutions@ GHR-Training.com to discuss your training or speaker needs and to receive detailed information about how we can *help you protect and optimize your greatest asset—your people!*

Ten Tips to Protect Against Harassment Charges

Tip #1: Create *a clear, zero-tolerance Harassment/Discrimination Policy.*

- Define and cover quid pro quo harassment.
- Define and cover hostile environment harassment.
- Stress the significance of effect, regardless of intent.
- Cover all bases of harassment and discrimination (e.g., sex, race, religion, national origin, age, disability, sexual orientation, etc.).
- Specify consequences (e.g., up to and including termination of employment) and establish a complaint procedure.

"Zero tolerance" does not mean uniform severe punishment regardless of the severity of the behavior. Rather it means to...

Tip #2: Evenhandedly enforce *your policy, without exception.*

If you determine that your policy has been violated, enforce that policy, regardless of the offender's position in the organization! (Easier said than done? Perhaps. But consider the legal and employee-relations consequences of doing otherwise.)

Tip #3: Implement *user-friendly harassment/ discrimination internal complaint and investigation procedures.*

- Provide multiple options for registering complaints; written, hotline, in-person (e.g., supervisor, senior manager, HR), and include at least one female and as much diversity as possible.
- Designate (and train) male/female teams for complaint investigation.

Tip #4: Communicate *the policy and procedures.*

- In writing: employee handbook, bulletin boards, e-mail, memos, organization's website
- Verbally: new hire orientation, department meetings, one-on-one
- Reinforce periodically with in-person statements by senior management and immediate supervisors

Tip #5: Train *all employees on:*

- The essence and scope of relevant laws and your policy
- How to refrain from all forms of harassment and discrimination
- How to respond (including complaint procedure) to harassment/discrimination

Tip #6: Train *all managers on:*

- Everything covered in the employee training
- The costs, their responsibilities, what to avoid, what to watch out for

- How to handle complaints, including how to document

Tip #7: *Thoroughly* investigate *all harassment complaints.*

Not all allegations of harassment are of equal merit or severity. The one absolute, however, is: *Never ignore* a harassment complaint, whether made formally or as an informal gripe.

- Listen to all parties concerned.
- Maintain confidentiality (to the extent possible).
- Communicate the results of the investigation to the complainant and the accused.
- Take appropriate action, for example, feedback, training, coaching, counseling, disciplinary action, and/or termination.

Tip #8: Protect *complainants, witnesses, and the accused from retaliation.*

- Not only formal retaliation by the employer, but also informal retaliation by employees, such as gossiping or shunning.
- You may want to consider an "in good faith" caveat; that is, fabricated complaints will not be tolerated and will be subject to disciplinary action. If so, carefully distinguish this from honest complaints made in good faith, which are found not to be in violation of law or policy.

Tip #9: Document *all of the aforementioned.*

You probably will not be able to prevent harassment/discrimination lawsuits or EEOC charges from being filed against your organization. But you can ensure a favorable finding. Our advice:

Do the right thing...and document it!

Tip #10: Stay *vigilant.*

- Constantly monitor your work environment.
- Periodically review policy and procedures to ensure compliance and effectiveness.

Ten Steps to Manage Workplace Violence

Step #1: *Assemble a crisis management team.*

Include:

- Senior management
- Security personnel
- Medical personnel
- Legal advisors
- Human resources

- Employee assistance program
- Public relations experts
- Local law enforcement
- Background investigators
- Violence assessment experts

Step #2: *Create a crisis management plan.*

Address:

- Policy
- Procedures
- Team members and roles
- Communication plan

- Public relations plan
- Logistics plan
- Professional contacts
- Recovery plan

Include detailed procedures—supported by training and rehearsal—specifying who does what and when. For example:

- How to restrain the perpetrator (and when to do so)

- Dealing with the perpetrator after the incident
- How to contain the incident...and evacuation protocols
- Notification of security staff and/or police
- Summoning of medical staff
- Communications during the incident and afterward
- Providing EAP support

Step #3: Establish a violence-protection policy.

- Clearly state the organization's stand on violent, disruptive, and threatening behaviors, as well as weapons in the workplace.
- Specify an incident and warning sign reporting process. (See Step #7.)
- Post the policy at entrances, employment office, and break areas...include in the Employee Handbook...and verbally communicate the policy during new employee orientation, in department meetings, and in training sessions.
- Consistently enforce.

Step #4: Train managers and employees.

Employee training coverage includes:

- Workplace violence awareness
- The warning signs of a dangerous employee/customer and the triggering events
- Their duty to report all incidents and warning signs, not just overt violence and threats
- How to de-escalate threatening situations
- How to protect themselves and coworkers when threatened
- Their responsibility to treat all people with respect and dignity

Manager training coverage includes all of the above, plus:

- Proper discipline and terminations

- Their role in response and crisis management
- How to detect the behavioral profile during interviews and reference checks

Step #5: Use proper employee-selection techniques.

The hiring process, which screens out the potentially violent or unstable, is an organization's first line of defense. This should include:

- Control by an objective and consistent third party, such as HR.
- Review of applications and résumés for behavioral problems, not just skills. For example:

    Gaps in employment/education history, job-hopping, and so on.

    Anything suspicious or inconsistent.

- Broad background checks (not just criminal record) for all jobs.
- Contacting prior employers (i.e., actual supervisors) for all jobs—probing character/behavior-related issues, not just dates of employment or skills.
- Drug and validated psychological testing.
- An in-depth interview of all candidates by HR (looking for behavioral problems) prior to job offer, including:

    Behavioral interview questions, such as, "Give an example of how you perform under stress."

    Careful probing of reason for leaving, actual supervisor name, title, responsibilities, dates, and issues identified in the application/résumé review.

- Effective screening of contract, temporary, and part-time workers.

Step #6: Standardize discipline and termination procedures.

- Preserve the involved employee's dignity
- Include tactful and safe handling of high-risk employees and situations

- Handle by an objective and consistent third party, such as HR

Step #7: Recognize signs of trouble...and ensure they are reported.

Constantly stay on the alert for warning signs and triggering events. Establish and communicate reporting and tracking processes:

- Report physical violence, verbal abuse, emotional outbursts, threats, strange behavior, and disrespect...not just physical accidents, injuries, and illnesses.
- Offer alternative channels (other than chain of command) for reporting. For example:

  Ombudsman-type managers who represent as much diversity as possible and are perceived by most employees as approachable

  An internal or external hotline, with confidentiality safeguards

Step #8: Investigate all threats, complaints, and red flags.

- Take all specific threats seriously...and find out more about vague threats.
- Pull together your crisis management team.
- Investigate and interview:

  Talk with the complainant or victim (actual or potential) as soon as possible after the danger has been identified or after an incident has occurred.

  Document what both you and the complainant/victim say. (It may be needed for litigation.)

  Document the threat itself and get statements from others who have heard or observed the perpetrator.

  Meet with the threatener or perpetrator, take his or her statement, confront him or her with other statements taken, and document everything that transpires.

Step #9: Take appropriate action.

- Communicate the investigation results with the complainant/victim and provide support.

    Offer the victim the opportunity for professional counseling and/or security protection.

    Ask the victim what he or she needs from you to increase his or her level of comfort/safety.

- Meet with the threatener or perpetrator again and apply the following as appropriate:

    Training, coaching, counseling, EAP-referral, disciplinary action, termination, arrest

- If appropriate, notify authorities in the community.

Step #10: Deal with the aftermath.

- Address your employees' reactions.
- Address your managers' concerns.
- Gather professional support.
- Arrange for proper communication.
- Reassess and improve preventive measures.

The Impending Leadership Crisis

Seventy-six million Americans, the Baby Boomers, are approaching retirement age. (You might say that this is the "Dawning of the Aging of Aquarius.") But only 44 million are in the pipeline to replace them.

As a consequence, within the next two to ten years, organizations across the United States, in virtually all sectors and industries, will face a potential leadership crisis!

For example:

- According to Taleo, a talent management consultancy, 500 of the largest *companies* can expect to lose 50 percent of their senior management in the next five years.

- According to the U.S. Office of Personnel Management (OPM) Director Linda Springer, 90 percent of about 6,000 *federal* executives will be eligible for retirement over the next 10 years.

- A 2005 survey commissioned by the Annie E. Casey Foundation found that 65 percent of *nonprofit* leaders are expected to leave their positions by 2009.

THE *SECRET* TO THE LEADERSHIP CRISIS

Frankly, this is not so much a "secret." If you give it just a moment's thought, the solution is obvious:

Identify and develop potential leaders (at all levels).

Hope you didn't think the secret was headhunting. The nature of the crisis is such that there aren't enough heads to hunt. What will distinguish the successful organizations from also-rans is actually doing it.

As we have said in a different, but related, context, every crisis contains not only danger, but also opportunity. Those organizations that have already undertaken this approach, will not just survive, but will flourish. They will have capitalized on their primary talent resource—their current employees—and be in a better position to pick leadership talent from other organizations.

Although it may already be a bit late to begin this process from scratch, organizations that do so will at least fare better than those that do nothing.

The Optimizing Contributions tools (see Tools #9–#12) reveal how to develop employees, including potential leaders. Here we explore how to *identify* those new leaders.

We propose nine essential traits (emphasizing three that are unique to leaders), describe four methods to spot the traits, disclose the underlying secret to revealing a leader's potential (what we call "The Harry Truman Factor"), and suggest an application for your own workplace.

THE TRAITS

You are a leader. So, why not look for someone just like you? Well, as you may realize, this would not enhance diversity and might lead to potential discrimination. Also, although many of your traits are relevant, many have nothing to do with leadership; and some of your traits may be counterproductive.

It is better to start with a blank sheet of paper and...

Determine the essential traits of leaders.

We've determined nine such traits. The first three are:

1. *Integrity*: Honest, congruent between word and deed, competent, trusted, respected

2. *Dedication*: Self-motivated, prepared to do whatever it takes, mentally tough

3. *Results*: Gets things done, goal-oriented, sets and achieves short-term goals, completes projects, has and/or encourages practical ideas

Although you might organize or label these traits differently, we expect that you would include these on your own list. We submit, however, that these traits are not unique to leaders. You want all of your employees—certainly your professionals—to possess such attributes. And that's how we classify this group: the *Professionals* traits.

The next three traits are:

4. *Responsibility*: "The buck stops here." Assumes responsibility, is accountable

5. *Vision*: A clearly defined sense of purpose and direction—setting it, dedicated to it, and communicating it; has a constructive spirit of discontent; innovates, embraces change; focuses on the long-range goal

6. *Decisions*: Decides quickly, displays confidence, acts independently when necessary, analyzes situations carefully, makes rational judgments and logical decisions, takes calculated risks

We think this group ratchets it up a notch. Leaders definitely need to possess such traits. But then, so do entrepreneurs (e.g., independent consultants like the authors). Thus, we classify these three as *Entrepreneurs* traits.

As you look at the list of six traits thus far, what element is missing? We submit that it is…interaction with *people*.

With that in mind, here are our final three—the traits unique to *Leaders*:

7. *Influence*: Develops strong working relationships, builds rapport quickly, strong team player, works effectively with people, expresses views clearly and with impact, politically savvy

8. ***Empowerment***: Works through others, delegates, sensitive to people's needs, involves others in plans and decisions, motivates, develops others, shares credit, listens

9. **Command**: Has presence and authority, enjoys being in charge, takes the lead, initiates

All nine traits are important, but anyone in your current workforce whom you would even consider for leadership development should already possess the first three *Professionals* traits.

So, focus instead on the traits unique to *Entrepreneurs* and, especially, *Leaders*.

SPOT THE TRAITS

Now that you've determined the traits to look for, how do you go about detecting them in your current employees (or in outsiders)?

There are four methods:

1. Examine previous experience (and outside activities)

2. Observe current behavior

3. Assessment instruments

4. 360-degree feedback

We regard the first two methods as essential. The other two are optional, but can be quite useful.

When examining *previous experience* (and outside activities), look at:

- What leadership positions (formal and informal) has the individual held?

- What leadership roles has he or she assumed (regardless of position)?

- How effective was he or she in those positions and roles?

- What traits (or their absence) did he or she demonstrate in those positions and roles?

- What traits (or their absence) has he or she demonstrated in non-leader roles?

Then look at *current behavior* ... ask the same kind of questions as when you examined previous experience:

- What leadership roles has the individual assumed in the current job?
- How effective is he or she in those roles?
- What traits (or their absence) is he or she demonstrating in those roles?
- What traits (or their absence) is he or she demonstrating in non-leader roles?

This should give you a good sense of whether the individual has what it takes to fill your shoes. But you can supplement this with a couple of other techniques:

Assessment instruments are questionnaires that rate the extent the individual displays the traits; both self-assessments and assessments completed by others.

These are available from many outside consultants (see the Resource Guide).

The results are often plotted on a four-quadrant matrix, as shown here.

For example, a leader needs to be strong in both task and people.

360-degree feedback is an assessment instrument completed by superiors, subordinates, peers, and self—thereby providing a complete 360-degree view of the individual.

These also are available from many outside consultants, such as, PDI's PROFILOR® and DDI's *Leadership Mirror®.*

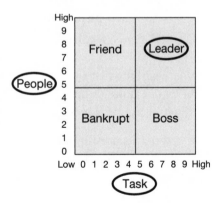

—————[**OPPORTUNITY**   ]—————

Trait spotting is a somewhat passive process. It is necessary, but not sufficient. You need to do more than just observe and assess.

There is an additional question to add to each method:

- Has he or she been given the *opportunity* to demonstrate these traits?

We call this "The Harry Truman Factor." During his brief vice presidency, the relatively unknown and untried Harry Truman stood in the shadows of charismatic President Franklin Delano Roosevelt. Upon Roosevelt's death, when Truman was thrust onto the world stage during the last year of World War II (that is, when he was given the opportunity), he demonstrated his own unique style of leadership and the ability to make the tough decisions (e.g., dropping the atom bomb and, during the Korean War, firing popular General Douglas MacArthur).

You may have noticed our use of Truman's trademark, "The buck stops here."

So...

**Provide your professionals the *opportunity*
to rise to the challenge.**

Make sure that your employees who exhibit the *Professionals* traits are given opportunities to demonstrate the other traits as well.

And remember the Autonomy Tip in Tool #2: "Difficult challenges—when coupled with the ability to make meaningful changes—create enthusiasm, loyalty, and peak performance"...and enable potential leaders to rise to the challenges.

APPLICATION

1. *Select* one employee who you think may have leadership potential.

2. For each *Leader* and *Entrepreneur* trait, ask *yourself:*

   - How has he or she *displayed* this trait?

   - How has he or she displayed the *absence* of this trait?

   - What *opportunities* does he or she need to express and/or practice this trait?

3. Start *providing* those opportunities to that person.

Resource Guide

INTRODUCTION: A TOOL KIT FOR TODAY'S WORKPLACE

Grimme, Don & Sheryl. *The Grimme Report.*
http://www.WorkplacePeopleSolutions.com/

Tulgan, Bruce. "Generational Shift: What We Saw at the Workplace Revolution." RainmakerThinking, September 17, 2003.
http://www.rainmakerthinking.com/rschrpts.htm

PART 1: LEADING PEOPLE

What Do Employees Want?

Grimme, Don & Sheryl. *Employee Retention Headquarters.*
http://www.Employee-Retention-HQ.com

Kaye, Beverly L., and Sharon Jordan-Evans. *Love 'Em or Lose 'Em: Getting Good People to Stay.* Berrett-Koehler, 2002.

Tool #1: Turn On Talent...and Turn Off Turnover

Bond, James T., et al. *The 1997 National Study of the Changing Workforce.* Families and Work Institute, No. 2, 1998.

Covey, Stephen R. *The 7 Habits of Highly Effective People.* Free Press, 2004.

Employee Turnover Trends 2007. TalentKeepers, 2007. www.TalentKeepers.com

"Equity Theory." *Wikipedia.* http://en.wikipedia.org/wiki/Equity_theory

Esen, Evren. "2005 U.S. Job Recovery and Retention Poll Findings." Society for Human Resource Management, November 2005.

"Executives Predict Employee Turnover Will Worsen in 2007." TalentKeepers, April 2007. http://www.talentkeepers-services.com/talentkeepers/news_view.asp?id=43

Fyock, Catherine. "SHRM White Paper: Retention Tactics That Work." Society for Human Resource Management, 1998.

Galinsky, Ellen, et al. "The Changing Workforce: Highlights of the [1992] National Study." Families and Work Institute, 1993.

"Kano Tutorial." C2C Solutions. http://www.c2c-solutions.com/kano_tutorial.htm

Koch, Jennifer. "Satisfy Them with More Than Money." *Workforce,* 1998.

Nelson, Bob. *1001 Ways to Reward Employees.* Workman Publishing, 1994.

Nelson, Bob. *1001 Ways to Energize Employees.* Workman Publishing, 1997.

Schramm, Jennifer. "SHRM Workplace Forecast." Society for Human Resource Management, 2006.

Spitzer, Dean R. *Supermotivation: A Blueprint for Energizing Your Organization from Top to Bottom.* AMACOM, 1995.

"Two Factor Theory." *Wikipedia.*
http://en.wikipedia.org/wiki/Two_factor_theory

Tool #2: Unleash Their Productivity

Buckingham, Marcus, and Curt Coffman, (The Gallup Organization). *First Break All the Rules.* Simon and Schuster, 1999.

"EAP Directory." *DataLink.* http://www.eap-sap.com/eap/index.html

Employee Assistance Professionals Association. http://www.eapassn.org

Galinsky, Ellen, et al. "Overwork in America...Executive Summary." Families and Work Institute, 2005. http://familiesandwork.org/site/research/summary/overwork2005summ.pdf

Herman, Roger, and Joyce Gioia. "The Herman Trend Alert." The Herman Group, Inc., March 18, 1998. http://www.hermangroup.com/alert/archive_3-18-98.html

Maslach, Christina, and Michael P. Leiter. *The Truth About Burnout: How Organizations Cause Personal Stress and What to Do About It.* Jossey-Bass, 1997.

Nanus, Burt. *Visionary Leadership.* Jossey-Bass, 1995.

O'Hallaron, Richard D. "The Mission Primer: Four Steps to an Effective Mission Statement." *Mission Incorporated,* 2000.

Ventrice, Cindy. *Make Their Day!: Employee Retention That Works.* Berrett-Koehler, 2003.

Wulfhorst, Ellen. "Americans Work More, Seem to Accomplish Less." Reuters, February 22, 2006.

Tool #3: Balance Their Work and Life

Bond, James T., et al. *Highlights of the [2002] National Study of the Changing Workforce.* Families and Work Institute, No. 3, 2002.

Employers for Work-Life Balance.
http://www.employersforwork-lifebalance.org.uk/

"Work-Life Balance." *Wikipedia.*
http://en.wikipedia.org/wiki/Work-life_balance

---[

PART 2:
DIFFERENT STROKES

]---

Individual Differences

Development Dimensions International (DDI). www.ddiworld.com

"DISC Profile." http://www.discprofile.com/

"The Keirsey Temperament Sorter (KTS)." http://www.keirsey.com/
The Myers and Briggs Foundation (MBTI). http://www.myersbriggs.org/

"The Personality Page." http://www.personalitypage.com/

Personnel Decisions International (PDI). www.personneldecisions.com

Wonderlic. http://www.wonderlic.com/

Tool #4: Embrace Diversity

Dana, Peter H. "Map Projection Overview." University of Colorado, 1994.
http://www.colorado.edu/geography/gcraft/notes/mapproj/mapproj.html

DeVaney, Carol-Susan, et al. *Workforce Diversity Participant's Book.* HRD
Press, 2003.

Loden, Marilyn. *Implementing Diversity: Best Practices for Making Diversity
Work in Your Organization.* McGraw-Hill, 1996.

Simons, George. *Working Together: Succeeding in a Multicultural
Organization.* Crisp, 1994.

Sonnenschein, William. *The Diversity Toolkit: How You Can Build and
Benefit from a Diverse Workforce.* McGraw-Hill, 1999.

U.S. Census Bureau. http://www.census.gov/

U.S. Department of Labor—Bureau of Labor Statistics.
http://www.bls.gov/

Tool #5: Get a Grip on Generations

Massey, Morris. *What You Are Is Where You Were When…AGAIN!*
training video, Enterprise Media, 2006. http://www.enterprisemedia.com

Lancaster, Lynne C., and David Stillman. *When Generations Collide: Who
They Are. Why They Clash. How to Solve the Generational Puzzle at Work.*
HarperCollins, 2003.

Zemke, Ron, et al. *Generations at Work: Managing the Clash of Veterans,
Boomers, Xers, and Nexters in Your Workplace.* AMACOM, 1999.

Tool #6: Focus on Ability

"ADA Home Page." U.S. Department of Justice. http://www.ada.gov/

"Disability Discrimination." U.S. Equal Employment Opportunity
Commission. http://www.eeoc.gov/types/ada.html

"Job Accommodation Network." Office of Disability Employment Policy—
U.S. Department of Labor. http://www.jan.wvu.edu/

The 10 Commandments of Communicating with People with Disabilities.
training video, Program Development Associates.
http://disabilitytraining.com/tcd.html, 800-543-2119

PART 3:
LEADER EFFECTIVENESS

Tool #7: Tell Them What Worked…and What Didn't

Blanchard, Kenneth H., and Spencer Johnson. *The One Minute Manager.*
HarperCollins Business, 2000.

"Giving Constructive Feedback." *Coaching & Mentoring For Dummies.*
Wiley Publishing.
http://www.dummies.com/WileyCDA/DummiesArticle/id-622.html

Tool #8: Ask Them...Then Listen

"Active Listening." *Wikipedia.* http://en.wikipedia.org/wiki/Active_listening

Bone, Diane. *The Business of Listening.* Axzo Press/Crisp, 1994.

Burley-Allen, Madelyn. *Listening: The Forgotten Skill.* Wiley, 1995.

Whitney, Diana, et al. *The Power of Appreciative Inquiry: A Practical Guide to Positive Change.* Berrett-Koehler, 2003.

PART 4: OPTIMIZING CONTRIBUTIONS

Tool #9: Diagnose Problems

Fournies, Ferdinand F. *Why Employees Don't Do What They're Supposed To Do and What To Do About It.* McGraw-Hill, 1999.

Tool #10: Coach the Good Ones...and the Not So Good

Fournies, Ferdinand F. *Coaching for Improved Work Performance.* McGraw-Hill, 1999.

Whitmore, John. *Coaching for Performance.* Nicholas Brealey, 2002.

Tool #11: Mentor the Great Ones

Brounstein, Marty. *Coaching and Mentoring for Dummies.* IDG Books Worldwide, 2000.

Johnson, W. Brad, and Charles R. Ridley. *The Elements of Mentoring.* Palgrave Macmillan, 2004.

Tool #12: Turn On Teamwork

Dressler, Larry. *Consensus Through Conversation: How to Achieve High-Commitment Decisions*. Berrett-Koehler, 2006.

Katzenbach, Jon R., and Douglas K. Smith. *The Wisdom of Teams: Creating the High-Performance Organization*. Collins, 2006.

Lencioni, Patrick M. *The Five Dysfunctions of a Team: A Leadership Fable*. Jossey-Bass, 2002.

Miller, Brian C. *Quick Teambuilding Activities for Busy Managers: 50 Exercises That Get Results in Just 15 Minutes*. AMACOM, 2004.

Streibel, Barbara J. *The Team Handbook Third Edition*. Oriel Incorporated, 2003.

PART 5: PERSONAL AND INTERERSONAL EFFECTIVENESS

Tool #13: Blow Away Burnout

Davis, Martha, et al. *Relaxation And Stress Reduction Workbook*. New Harbinger Publications, 2000.

Galinsky, Ellen, et al. "Overwork in America…Executive Summary." Families and Work Institute, 2005. http://familiesandwork.org/site/research/summary/overwork2005summ.pdf

Kabat-Zinn, Jon. *Full Catastrophe Living: Using the Wisdom of Your Body and Mind to Face Stress, Pain, and Illness*. Delta, 1990.

Potter, Beverly A. *Overcoming Job Burnout: How to Renew Enthusiasm for Work*. Ronin Publishing, 2005.

Sauter, Steven, et al. "STRESS…At Work." National Institute for Occupational Safety and Health. http://www.cdc.gov/niosh/stresswk.html

"Serenity Prayer." *Wikipedia.* http://en.wikipedia.org/wiki/Serenity_Prayer

Tool #14: Stay On Top of Stress

Rand, Ayn. "The Metaphysical Versus the Man-Made." *Philosophy: Who Needs It.* Signet, 1984.

Tool #15: Accentuate the Positive

Helmstetter, Shad. *What to Say When You Talk to Yourself.* Pocket, 1990.

Matt, Michele, CSP. *Attitude: The Choice Is Yours.* Book Marketing Solutions, 2007.

Peale, Norman Vincent. *The Power of Positive Thinking.* Fawcett, 1981.

Tool #16: Assert Yourself...and Deal with "Difficult" People

Attacking Anxiety. Midwest Center for Stress and Anxiety, 1989. http://www.stresscenter.com, call 800-944-9460 for free information about Lucinda Bassett's Attacking Anxiety and Depression Program.

Branden, Nathaniel. *Self Esteem at Work.* Jossey-Bass, 1998.

Paterson, Randy J. *The Assertiveness Workbook: How to Express Your Ideas and Stand Up for Yourself at Work and in Relationships.* New Harbinger Publications, 2000.

Wodarski, John S., and Marvin D. Feit. *Adolescent Substance Abuse.* Haworth Press, 1995.

Tool #17: Own Your Anger...Don't Let It Own You

Brigman, Greg, and Barbara Earley Goodman. *Group Counseling for School Counselors.* Walch Publishing, 2001.

Gentry, W. Doyle. *Anger Management For Dummies.* Wiley, 2006.

Tool #18: Rise to the Challenge of Change

Charles, C. Leslie. *Why is Everyone So Cranky?: The Ten Trends Complicating Our Lives and What We Can Do About Them.* Hyperion, 2001.

Herbert, Frank. *Dune.* Ace, 1990.

Jeffers, Susan. *Feel the Fear and Do It Anyway.* Fawcett Columbine, 1987.

PART 6: ELIMINATING CONFLICT

Tool #19: Prevent All Forms of Harassment

"Harassment." The U.S. Equal Employment Opportunity Commission. http://www.eeoc.gov/types/harassment.html

"Harassment." *Wikipedia.* http://en.wikipedia.org/wiki/Harassment

Tool #20: Prevent Workplace Violence

American Institute on Domestic Violence. http://www.aidv-usa.com/

de Becker, Gavin. *The Gift of Fear.* Dell, 1997.

Grimme, Don & Sheryl. *Workplace Violence Headquarters.* http://www.Workplace-Violence-HQ.com

Gurchiek, Kathy. "Workplace Violence Is on the Upswing, Say HR Leaders." *HR Magazine,* July 2005. http://newsmanager.commpartners.com/hrma/issues/2005-05-25/12.html

Kelleher, Michael D. *New Arenas for Violence: Homicide in the American Workplace.* Praeger/Greenwood, 1996.

McClure, Lynne F. *Risky Business: Managing Employee Violence in the Workplace.* Haworth Press, 1996.

"Occupational Violence." National Institute for Occupational Safety and Health. http://www.cdc.gov/niosh/topics/violence/

"Seung-Hui Cho." *Wikipedia.* http://en.wikipedia.org/wiki/Seung-Hui_Cho

"Violence and Theft in the Workplace." Bureau of Justice Statistics—U.S. Department of Justice. http://www.ojp.usdoj.gov/bjs/pub/press/thefwork.pr

"Violence in the Workplace." NIOSH. http://www.cdc.gov/niosh/violcont.html

"Workplace Violence, 1992–1996." Bureau of Justice Statistics—U.S. Department of Justice. http://www.ojp.usdoj.gov/bjs/abstract/wv96.htm

"Workplace Violence Survey Results." Risk Control Strategies. http://www.riskcontrolstrategies.com/workplace_violence_survey.htm

Tool #21: Defuse and Protect

Chavez, Larry J. "Workplace Violence 101." Critical Incident Associates. http://www.workplace-violence.com/

Dealing with Workplace Violence—A Guide for Agency Planners. U.S. Office of Personnel Management, February 1998. http://www.opm.gov/employment_and_benefits/worklife/officialdocuments /handbooksguides/workplaceviolence/full.pdf

Rugala, Eugene A., and Arnold R. Isaacs. *Workplace Violence: Issues in Response.* FBI Academy, 2004. http://www.fbi.gov/publications/violence.pdf

"Safety and Health Topics: Workplace Violence." Occupational Safety and Health Administration. http://www.osha.gov/SLTC/workplaceviolence/index.html

Afterword

Grimme, Don & Sheryl. *GHR Training Solutions.* http://www.GHR-Training.com

Appendix C: The Impending Leadership Crisis

Clark, Donald. "Leadership Questionnaire." January 13, 2007.
http://www.nwlink.com/~donclark/leader/matrix.html

Gregoire, Michael. "Consistently Acquiring and Retaining Top Talent."
Taleo. http://www.taleo.com/news/consistently-acquiring-and-retaining-top-talent.php

Kunreuther, Frances. *Up Next: Generation Change and the Leadership of Nonprofit Organizations.* Annie E. Casey Foundation, 2005.
http://www.aecf.org/upload/PublicationFiles/LD2928K643.pdf

Leadership Mirror®. Development Dimensions International (DDI).
www.ddiworld.com

PROFILOR®. Personnel Decisions International. (PDI).
www.personneldecisions.com

Springer, Linda, and Nancy H. Kichak. "Retirees Returning to the Rescue: Re-Employing Annuitants in Times of National Need."
U.S. Office of Personnel Management, July 25, 2006.
https://www.opm.gov/news_events/congress/testimony/7_25_2006.asp

Index

ability
  focus on, 68, 77
  individual differences in, 38–39
  performance problems and, 100
  see also Americans with Disabilities Act (ADA)
access, 74
accommodation, 35–36, *see also* Americans
  with Disabilities Act (ADA); reasonable
  accommodation
active listening, 90–95
  assertion and, 159
  grievances and, 216
  importance of, 22
affirmative action, 42–43
African Americans
  stereotypes concerning, 53–54, 56
  in the workforce, 48–49, 53–54
aggression, 154–155, 167, 181
Alcoholics Anonymous (AA), 177
Americans with Disabilities Act (ADA), 39,
  65–77
anger, 87, 121, 161–171
applications, job, 75
appreciation, 6–8, 19
appropriate language, 67
Asians
  stereotypes concerning, 54
  in the workforce, 48–49, 54

assertion, 87–88, 120–121, 151–160
assumptions, challenging, 68
attitude, 120, 134–150, 141–142
authority, stress and, 137
autonomy of employees, 30–31

Baby Boomers, 58, 60–63
  gender of workforce and, 48
  pending leadership crisis and, 232–237
Barton, Mark, 202
Baruch, Bernard M., 41
behavioral anger, 164
behavior disorders, 70
Beth Israel Hospital, 16–17
Blacks, *see* African Americans
Blanchard, Kenneth, 83
Boomers, *see* Baby Boomers
bosses, stress and, 137
brainstorming, 117–118
breathing exercises, 127–128, 159, 192
Brigman, Greg, 169–171
burnout, 29–30, 120, 123–132

C2C Solutions, 12
career frustration, 207
caring for employees, 35
celebrating successes, 23–24
"challenging situations," 159

Chan, Charlie, 54
Chan, Jackie, 54
change, 172–177
Chavez, Larry, 215–217
children, anger and, 167
Cho, Seung-Hui, 200, 202, 205, 206, 209–211
Circle of Imagination, 147–148
Civil Rights Act of 1964, 65, 184–185, 186, 187
client harassment, 186
Clinton, Hillary, 54, 55
coaching, 96, 103–109, 113
Colin, Sam, 20
Columbine High School shooting incident, 205–206, 207, 209–212
communication
  about abilities, 77
  active listening and, 22, 90–95, 159, 216
  about anger, 165–168
  of attitude, 141–142
  among generations, 63–64
  of goals, 19
  inquiry in, 89–95
  of mission and vision, 28–29
  opening two-way, 78–79
  in protecting against harassment charges, 224
  self-talk in, 144–147
  sharing information with employees, 23
  between supervisors and employees, 3
conceptual package deals, 136–137
conflict, 178
confrontation, avoiding, 215
consensus, team building and, 117–118
constructive feedback, 19, 81, 83–88, 90
core attributes, 44
core competencies, 28
Critical Incident Associates, 215–217
critic approach, 140–141
criticism, 19
CSI (TV show), 53
culture fit, 30

de Becker, Gavin, 197–198
defusing anger, 165
demonstrating instructions, 36
depression, 124
development coaching, 104
"difficult" people, 158–160
disability, as term, 69–71
disciplining employees, 219–220
discrimination, 66, 74, see also stereotypes

diversity, 41–56
  dimensions of, 43–46
  individual differences and, 38–39
  myth and reality, 42–43
  perceptions and preconceptions concerning, 46–48, 51–53
  riddle concerning, 50–51
  stereotypes and, 53–56
  trends in, 48–49
DOGS (defusing of grievance=safety), 215–217

earnings and benefits, 12–14, 16
emotional anger, 164
Employee Assistance Program (EAP), 31–32
employee harassment, 186
employees
  active listening to, 22, 90–95, 159, 216
  autonomy to deal with challenges, 30–31
  celebrating successes of, 23–24
  communication between supervisors and, 3
  creating opportunities for, 21–22
  disciplining, 66, 74, 219–220
  grievances of, 215–217
  hiring process, 74–76, 208
  involving in plans and decisions, 20–21
  linking mission and job to talents and aspirations of, 29–30
  as material versus human resources, 1–2
  motivation of, 8, 9–24, 101
  performance problems of, 71, 99–104, 109
  productivity of, 8, 25–32
  protecting against harassment charges, 224
  reciprocity with, 31–32
  retention of, 8, 9–24
  sharing information with, 23
  stress and, 137
  training of, 100, 224–225
  what employees want, 6–8, 17, 23
equal access, 73–74
Equal Employment Opportunity Commission (EEOC), 187–188
Equity Theory, 16
escalating anger, 170–171
essential job functions, 71
Eurocentrism, 47–48
excitement needs, 12
expectations
  generations and, 61–62
  performance problems and, 100

expressing anger, 167–168
external stress, 134

Families and Work Institute, National Study
     of the Changing Workforce, 13–14,
     21–35, 123–124, 133
family issues, 36
faulty thinking, stress and, 134–137
favoritism, avoiding, 35
fear, 197–198
   attitude and, 148–149
   challenging, 68
   change and, 173–174
feedback
   anger and, 168
   combining positive and constructive,
     85–87
   constructive, 19, 81, 83–88, 90
   as continuous and interactive process, 81
   positive, 82, 85–87
   two-way communication and, 78–79
Feel the Fear Do It Anyway (Jeffers),
     173–174
Feit, Marvin, 156–157
flexibility, 177
flexible work arrangements, 34–35
Four Arenas of Attack, 127–132, 150
furiousness, anger and, 163

Gallup Organization, 8
generations, 57–64
   communication among, 63–64
   conflict between, 62–63
   expectations of, 61–62
   list of, 58
   shared experiences of, 58–61
   values of, 61–62
Generation X (Gen X), 58–63
Gift of Fear, The (de Becker), 197–198
goals
   communicating to employees, 19
   linking employee and organizational, 21–22
Gone With the Wind (film), 53
Goodman, Barbara Earley, 169–171
Graham, Gerald, 19
Greatest Generation, *see* Traditionalists
Greenspan, Alan, 55
grievances, 215–217
Grimme 3-Factor Theory, 8, 12, 13–15
groups, 115–116

harassment, 74, 181–196, 223–226
   as abuse of power, 181
   defined, 181
   examples of, 188–190
   legal aspects of, 184–185
   protecting against charges, 223–226
   responding to, 191
   role as line manager and, 191–193
   scenarios, 193–196
   scope of, 186–187
   secret basis of, 187–188
   sexual harassment, 182–186
   tips to protect against, 186, 190, 196
Harding, Tonya, 115–116, 142–143, 149
Harris, Eric, 205–207
Hawking, Stephen, 68
health problems, 75–76, 124, *see also*
     Americans with Disabilities Act
     (ADA)
Herbert, Frank, 173–174
Hershey Foods, 21
Herzberg, Frederick, 12
Hewitt Associates, 24
Hewlett-Packard, 18
high-performance teams, 116
Hill, Anita, 186
hiring process, 74–76, 208
Hitler, Adolf, 212
Hughes, Sarah, 142, 143, 149
Hurricane Katrina, 10–11, 56
Hurricane Wilma, 11
hygiene factors (Herzberg), 12

Illinois Task Force, 185
immediate supervisors, 3
immigrants, in the workforce, 48–49
individual differences, 38–39
inquiry, 89–95
internal stress, 134
interpersonal arena, burnout in, 129
interviews, job, 75
involvement, employee desire for, 6–8

Jeffers, Susan, 173–174
job demands, 8, 12–14, 26–27, 31, 33
job descriptions, 74
job design, performance problems and,
     100
job quality, 12–14, 26, 27, 28–32, 33
Johnson, Spencer, 83

Kano Model of Customer Service, 12–13
Katzenbach, John R., 115–116
Kelleher, Michael D., 204–205
Kerrigan, Nancy, 115–116, 143–144
Kinsey, Alfred, 43
Klebold, Dylan, 205–206
Kovach, Ken, 7
Kwan, Michelle, 142

Latinos, 48–49
leadership
  leader, defined, 3
  pending crisis in, 232–237
  requirements of, 3
  responsibilities of workplace leaders, 73–74
  stress and, 135–136
  traits of leaders, 233–236
  what employees want, 6–8, 17, 23
  workplace leaders, 3
Leiter, Michael, 29–30
letting go of anger, 168–169
Li, Jet, 54
life skills, 120–121
lifestyle of employees, 30
Lindahl, Lawrence, 7
listening, active, 22, 90–95, 159, 216
Litany Against Fear, 173–174
Lockheed Martin, 199, 200, 212–213
Loden, Marilyn, 43
loner personalities, 206
loss, change and, 174
loyalty, stress and, 137

Make Their Day! (Ventrice), 30
managers
  attitudes toward employees, 1–2
  protecting against harassment charges, 224–225
  role of line managers, 191–193
manipulation, 155
marginal (nonessential) job functions, 71
Martin, Casey, 65–66, 69, 71–72
Maslach, Christina, 29–30
Maslow Hierarchy of Needs, 10–12
Massey, Morris, 57
McClure, Lynne, 208
media, generations and, 59
medical exams and history, 75–76
mellowness, anger and, 163
mental anger, 164

mental arena, burnout in, 128–129
mentoring, 96, 105–106, 110–113
Mercator projections, 47–48, 51
Miami Baptist Hospital, 24
micromanagement, 136
Millennials (Gen Y), 58–64
Mirage Hotel (Las Vegas), 22, 31
mission, 28–30
Mollweide equal area projection, 47
motivation of employees, 8, 9–24, 101
Motorola, 22, 23, 28
Myers-Briggs Type Indicator (MBTI), 39

National Study of the Changing Workforce
  (Families and Work Institute), 13–14,
  21–35, 123–124, 133
Native Americans, 48–49
negative attitude, 141, 142, 144, 145
Nelson, Bob, 15–16, 31
neutral attitude, 141, 142, 144
New Arenas for Violence (Kelleher),
  204–205
nonverbal harassment, 189
numbness, anger and, 163

1001 Ways to Energize Employees (Nelson), 31
One Breath Rule, 192
One-Minute Manager, The (Blanchard and
  Johnson), 83

Parilla, Ralph, 181
Parks, Rosa, 153
passive-aggression, 155
passivity, 154–155
perceptions, 46–48, 51–53
performance evaluations, 74
performance needs, 12
performance problems, 71, 99–104, 109
personal issues, 36
personality
  individual differences in, 39
  in POSTAL model for predicting violence,
    206–207
  vulnerability to stress and, 137–138
Peterson, Steve, 17
physical anger, 164
physical arena, burnout in, 127–128
player approach, 140–141
policy, stress and, 137
pop culture, generations and, 61

positive attitude, 141, 142, 146–150, 176, 177
positive feedback, 82, 85–87
POSTAL model for predicting violence,
    203–213
  applying the profile, 208
  behavioral characteristics in, 206–207
  case study in, 204–207
  hiring process and, 208
  observable warning signs, 203, 208–211, 212
  profile, described, 203, 205–207
  shotgun, 203, 211
  triggering events, 203, 211–212
potentially offensive harassment, 189–190
potential teams, 116
praise, 17–20, 82
preconceptions, 46–48, 51–53
prejudgment, challenging, 68
present tense, positive attitude and, 147–148
Productive Pat, 106–107, 113
productivity of employees, 8, 25–32
  earnings and benefits and, 12–14, 16
  job demands and, 12–14, 26–27, 31, 33
  job quality and, 12–14, 26, 27, 28–32, 33
  workplace support and, 14, 26, 27, 33
pseudo teams, 115
Publix Super Markets, 17, 23
purifying breath exercise, 127–128

qualified, as term, 71–72

Radio Babies, see Traditionalists
Rainmaker Thinking Inc., 3
Rand, Ayn, 136–137
real teams, 115–116
reasonable accommodation, 67, 72–73,
    see also Americans with Disabilities Act
    (ADA)
reciprocity with employees, 31–32
Reeve, Christopher, 68
reframing, 135–136, 146–147, 159
rejecting change, 174–175
relaxation, 131–132
respect, 2–3, 16–17
retention of employees, 8, 9–24
Rice, Condoleezza, 55
Risky Business (McClure), 208
Rockin' Robin, 107–108, 113

safety-related concerns, 76
safety/security needs, 11, 12

St. Paul Fire and Marine Insurance Co., 124
same-sex harassment, 186–187
Sandwich Technique, 85–87
SARAH, 175–176
Scripps Mercy Hospital (San Diego), 31
secondary attributes, 44
self-actualization needs, 11, 12
self-esteem
  assertion and, 155
  needs for, 11, 12
self-fulfilling prophecy, 54–55
self-identification, 76
self-neglect, 124
self-talk, 144–147
Serenity Prayer, 128, 169, 175, 177
Sex and the City (TV show), 53
sexual harassment, see harassment
sexual orientation, 44, 71, 187
Sherrill, Patrick, 199, 204–207, 209–211
"shoulds," 149
significant events, generations and, 59–61
Silent Generation, see Traditionalists
Slutskaya, Irena, 142
Smith, Douglas K., 115–116
social/belonging needs, 11, 12
social change, generations and, 60
Society for Human Resource Management
    (SHRM), 9, 10
spectator approach, 140–141
spiritual arena, burnout in, 130–132
Spitzer, Dean, 19
stereotypes, 53–56
stress, 120, 124, 133–138
  constructive purging of tension, 166
  positive attitude and, 176
stuffing anger, 170
submission, 154–155
successes, celebrating, 23–24
support system, 12–14, 26, 27, 33, 177
survival needs, 10–11, 12

TalentKeepers, 9, 10
talents of employees, 30–31
team building, 96, 114–119
technology, generations and, 59
Telemetrics International, 142–143
temperament of employees, 30
10 Commandments of Communicating with
    People with Disabilities (video), 77
terminating employees, 219–220

testing, job, 75
Thomas, Clarence, 186
3-Factor Theory (Grimme), 8, 12, 13–15
tradition, challenging, 69
Traditionalists, 58–63
training
  performance problems and, 100
  in protecting against harassment charges, 224–225
Treasure Island Hotel (Las Vegas), 31
Truth About Burnout, The (Maslach and Leiter), 29–30
two-way communication, 78–79

U.S. Figure Skating Team, 115–116, 142–144
U.S. Olympic Hockey Team, 116

values, generations and, 61–62
vendor harassment, 186
Ventrice, Cindy, 30
verbal harassment, 188–189
Verizon Wireless, 23–24
violence, *see* workplace violence
Virginia Tech shooting incident, 200, 202, 205–206, 210
vision, communicating, 28–29

Wagner, Robin, 142
Wayne, John, 54
weapons, coping with threats, 217–219
What You Are Is Where You Are (Massey), 57

white males
  stereotypes concerning, 53–54, 55
  in the workforce, 49, 53–54
Wilson, Valerie, 7
win-win resolutions, 216–217
Wisdom of Teams, The (Katzenbach and Smith), 115–116
Wodarski, John S., 156–157
women
  stereotypes concerning, 54, 55
  in the workforce, 48–49
Woods, Tiger, 38, 66
work environment
  performance problems and, 100–101
  violence in, *see* workplace violence
working groups, 115
work/life balance, 8, 33–37, 61, 95
workplace support, 12–14, 26, 27, 33
workplace violence, 197–213
  cautions concerning, 207–208
  coping with weapon threats, 217–219
  defusing hostile coworkers or customers, 214–217
  disciplining employees, 219–220
  managing, 227–231
  myths concerning, 199–200
  nature and scope of, 201–202
  POSTAL model for predicting, 203–213
  preventing, 212–213
  risk factors for, 202–203
  scenarios, 220–221
  terminating employees, 219–220
  trends in, 198–199

Xerox, 199